HOPE

IN SMALL DOSES

NIKKI STERN

RUTHENIA PRESS
Princeton, NJ

Ruthenia Press
445 Sayre Drive
Princeton, NJ 08540
(609) 951-0492

ISBN: 978-0-578-16068-9
Editors: Marly Cornell, Luis Granados
Photography: Cherie Siebert [www.artsfish.com]
Cover Design: Deborah Stern

Forward

Can anyone resolve the meaning of life, find the perfect connections between brain physiology and human emotion and adjudicate whether free will is reality or illusion in 150 or so pages? Of course not, but Nikki Stern sets us on the path in a book sparkling with observations, human dramas, and plenty of quandaries. Drawing on medical literature about pain and aging, art from Hesiod's poetic take on Pandora's Box to the film *Men In Black's* comic take on the shape of the cosmos, and speculations of secularists and an occasional theist, Nikki explores the rather awesome persistence of "hope."

This is not about the guarantee of reward in the afterlife or the pernicious falsehood of thinking we can all mold the world to our rational manipulation alone. It is a hard fought effort to "believe what is best about the human spirit," a dogged determination to figure out how, in a world without certainty, each of us must hope (and work and play) as if our lives mattered. Because, as Nikki reminds us, they do!

The Rev. Barry W. Lynn, Esq.
Executive Director, Americans United for Separation of Church and State

For Jim, who loved the life he had.

CONTENTS

Introduction

"Hope in small doses. What does that even mean?" Isn't that the first thing a reader might ask upon hearing that title? Would I need to add a subtitle? Provide an oral or written explanation? Include a disclaimer?

None of the above, as it turns out. Hope-seekers are smart people. Most of those I asked had an idea where I was going with the concept even before they saw the chapter titles, read the opening paragraphs, took in Cherie Siebert's stunning photography (ooh, pictures) or realized how compact the book is (ooh, short).

Others weren't sure what I meant, but they were nevertheless curious enough to pick up a copy.

Why an updated version? Not two decades into the 21st century, we are more than ever in need of a collective outlook informed neither by inflexible certainty nor soul-sucking cynicism; one that recognizes setbacks, plans for disappointment and still manages to hold its head up. Everyone will have his or her own idea about hope and its value, of course. But I suspect—I hope—whoever is reading this book is ready to try a new approach or improve upon a familiar one.

In any event, welcome.

Nikki Stern
April, 2015

Hope makes a good breakfast but a bad supper.
- Francis Bacon

CHAPTER 1

To Hope or Not to Hope

Hope, deceitful as it is, serves at least to lead us to the end of our lives by an agreeable route.
–Francois Duc de la Rochefoucauld

Hope. The word fairly quivers with possibility. We might, it could, perhaps, what if, why not? Don't stop; keep going; what have we got to lose? Imagine, hope urges us. We do. Hope builds nations, inspires explorers, rescues the depressed, lifts up the miserable, at least if centuries of writers, thinkers, poets, philosophers, and psychologists are to be believed.

Lovely as that sounds, it doesn't answer the question: What precisely is hope? An emotion? A belief? An instinct? Learned behavior?

It's all these and more—or less, depending on what you read and whom you believe. In English, the word is burdened with multiple meanings and restrictions, until very recently, on its use as an adverb. The Associated Press Stylebook, "the journalist's bible," has come around, declaring via Twitter that it now supports the contemporary usage of hopefully.[1] Since I'd been breaking that particular grammar rule for years, I greeted the announcement with relief.

The English language is guided by rules and confounded by exceptions to those rules. Words have multiple uses or overlapping meanings. Hope is just one example. "Who cares?" you may be asking. Yet trying to understand hope is critical to understanding how it might work in our lives, regardless of who we are, where we live, or where we are along our birth-to-death journey. Moreover, research continues to show that being able to experience hope is integral to living well.[2]

I learn, as many of us do, by asking questions. One that occurs to me is whether hope can work in the life of someone who questions so much.

If it's possible to be born a skeptic, I was. I wanted something to believe in; I just couldn't figure out what it should be. I had a vivid imagination that was sparked as much by dark possibilities as fairy tales. I saw not dead people but fiery crashes and watery graves, falling trees and swinging swords, wolves with red eyes and sharp teeth, imprisoned princesses and lost children. The Grimm versions of the classic tales made more sense to me than their Disney counterparts.

Though I distrusted conventional happy endings, I yearned for them. I wanted a life that was secure and exciting, adventurous, but also anchored by one true love and a place to call home. I dreamed of romance and marriage, and a career as a successful artist and philanthropist. I kept adjusting those dreams over the course of a lifetime. The career became less about renown than respect, the image of Prince Charming less about being perfect and more about being loyal and true. I did feel my life might work out favorably overall. Maybe I "hoped" it would.

Even as a child, I doubted a version of hope that looked like a greeting card, all flowers and rainbows and laughing children and woodland animals with big eyes. I knew that sort of hope was a fantasy: a miasma of unrealistic expectations and unsubstantiated beliefs, a magic place where everything works out for the best because the cosmos is inclined toward beneficence. Most adults don't see the world that way; I just grew suspicious earlier. Yet we're all prone (some might say vulnerable) to feelings of hope. Those feelings, as it turns out, take many forms.

Many of us equate hope with religion, or the belief in a supreme entity with a plan that we mere mortals can't understand.

The devout have faith that this entity will see to our welfare and reward us accordingly in the afterlife. No matter how terrible or inexplicable our present circumstances might be, there is sense in what is happening. Believers surrender to the superior goodness or wisdom of the plan, or whoever made it. There may be doubts along the way; but that sort of hope ultimately comes from the certainty that whatever happens, it's all for the best.

A second version of hope depends not so much on any identified deity, but rather on an unshakable conviction that we have absolute control over our own destinies. Life coaches and some therapists emphasize a form of hope that is the manifestation of our desires. In that paradigm, whatever we want will come to us if we simply learn to harness our internal energies and direct them in a particular fashion. The method evokes a sort of "if you want it, it will come" scenario.

What these versions of hope seem to have in common is their emphasis on predictability, on the *certainty* that belief in the power of either our own minds or a higher authority will yield a positive outcome. This is faith as expectation, mixed in, perhaps, with no small amount of entitlement. We *will* be rewarded for good behavior, i.e., for thinking correctly or believing fully.

For skeptics like me, absolute certainty is anathema; and any faith that turns on a rigid doctrine rather than on critical inquiry isn't one I'm likely to embrace. I'm inclined to look—and look and look—before I leap, whether the topic is politics, entertainment, or the latest *absolutely true* piece of information my best friend or search engine puts in front of me. It's not that I believe everything can be explained through deductive reasoning; I don't. I accept the unknowable, just as I accept my place in the cosmos (minor, miraculous, and less than fully comprehendible) with an attendant amount of awe and reverence. This mindset imposes its own requirements. I feel duty-bound to try to overcome my petty concerns and selfish impulses (although I don't always succeed) so that I might both appreciate human existence and perhaps add to it.

To embrace with conviction a better future in the face of adversity, the faithful might insist, is to display courage. I go along with that notion to a degree. Yet the kind of hope that depends exclusively on an external force easily morphs into passivity. The emphasis is on waiting. We wait for fate or fortune or some movement of the universe to make something happen: to change the world, fix the economy, heal (or take) a sick relative, hand out some sort of reward, or exact some sort of punishment. The upward-facing patience of the truly pious can be inspiring but hope as an exercise in wait-and-see doesn't do much of anything for me or, I suspect, many others.

Then there's activist hope. The opposite of the submissive version, it's based on the conviction that we can make a difference. There are those, both religious and secular, who believe they have a moral duty to make the world a better place. The former see it as a directive from God, the latter as the only way to live in fellowship with other human beings. Activist hope fueled Barack Obama's 2008 campaign and informed his slogan "Yes, we can." Notwithstanding the presumed religious source of Obama's inspiration, many people saw his hope as a secular call to arms. We don't wait passively for the universe or the higher power to act—or for our candidate to get elected, or our schools to get better. We do something.

Hope with teeth.

Activist hope doesn't appear to need divine encouragement, which might make it work for questing skeptics or other manner of human-centric individual. At the 2014 Secular Conference, human rights activist Gita Sahgal suggested such hope might even conquer fear.[3] Certainly the idea that dedicating oneself to *doing* something about the world's ills might create a sense of purpose. Purpose would appear to be an excellent way of staving off at least the fear that one can't effect change.

At the same time, we know, or should know, that even an activist version of hope won't necessarily produce the desired results. Effort *ought* to be rewarded. The truth is: it often isn't.

Some of my favorite social commentators are those who come down hard on unreasonable optimism and/or lazy thinking. Barbara Ehrenreich, author of *Bright-Sided: How Positive Thinking Is Undermining America*, declares in her book, "The threats that we face, individually and collectively, won't be solved by wishful thinking but by a clear-eyed commitment to taking action in the world."[4] Ehrenreich isn't endorsing activist hope, by the way. Fairly early in her book, she sends hope packing, dismissing it as nothing more than an uncontrollable emotion.

Whether hope is intuitive or learned, we still can't guarantee that feeling hopeful will make things better. This places hope in a precarious position. On one hand, we may work hard to reach our goals—home ownership or higher education for our children—only to see the opportunities dissolve. On the other, illness, loss, and fear of our mortality may cause us to embrace an irrational hope born of our desperation, one that ignores biological or medical realities. Neither outlook leaves us with much to look forward to in this life.

No wonder some see hope as the consummate trickster, leading us to higher ground only to shove us off a cliff, assuring us of a painful (or fatal) landing...and laughing all the way.

What's the point? Why hope? There's too much evil in the world, too much which can and does turn out for the worst. We do what we can, try and make the best of it, but sometimes fate or random events intervene and things don't work out. We can love, admire, respect, hang out with friends, or enjoy ourselves at any given moment. We can raise children, experience pleasure, help our neighbors, or engage in meaningful work. We can even commit ourselves to a better world. Can't we do all those things without hope?

Besides, aren't we all hoping, every time we think, "Maybe I can make this work"? Naysayers will dispute that observation. Even my childhood friend's grandmother was always qualifying her rare bursts of optimism. "Looking at you two, I could almost feel hopeful," she'd say, before adding something like, "but when I look at what's going on in the world"—here she'd wave her hand in a dismissive gesture—"feh!"—which we took to mean she didn't really see much to hope after all.

Some people will insist hope is irrelevant, impossible, illogical, or beside the point. Others are so consumed by despair that hope appears inaccessible. Neurological and psychological studies have focused on this group in developing cognitive therapies that might alter brain chemistry.[5] The idea is to pull patients out of depressive states by teaching them to hope. In reality, the patients are learning to look forward. Hope is the mechanism by which their sense of purpose is restored.

Unfortunately, cognitive-based therapy has been cheapened by efforts of some members of the "motivational industry." These attitude therapists and life coaches have recast the notion of positive psychology as a lifestyle choice that promises total control. Ehrenreich is especially enraged at those who insist on promoting the "positive" aspects of being a breast cancer survivor (she is one). She feels the awareness campaigns have put a happy face on the disease, which ends up pressuring the survivors to be upbeat at all times.

The most prominent recent example of positive psychology promotion is the 2006 book sensation, *The Secret*. Authored by an Australian life coach named Rhonda Byrne, *The Secret* recycles the age-old idea that what you put out comes back to you. Its arrival coincided with the zenith of Oprah Winfrey's influence. Winfrey fiercely promoted the book on her popular daytime talk show. *The Secret* appeared to support her goal of helping women overcome a victim mentality.

The book also supports a darker view about the consequences of failure. If bad things are happening to you, what you've put out to the universe must have been bad. In other words, you get what you deserve. It's an outrageous message to send to rape victims, terminally ill patients, or those trapped in conflict zones around the world. Indeed, Byrne gives passing reference to incidences of genocide by talking about "negative energy" that may be to blame. The book precept may not be new, but it peddles the illusion that we can manage outcomes by changing our energy. It also perpetrates the notion that victims are nothing more than people with bad karma.

What a negative, mean-spirited version of positive thinking that turns out to be.

I'm not sure human nature necessarily leads us to want what we can't get, but it does cause us to want *something*. We're a restless species. There's nothing wrong with dreams and desires, and our penchant for exploration and discovery is a wonderful aspect of our humanity. But wanting something doesn't automatically mean we'll get it. There's no magic bullet, although it appears to be human nature to want desperately to believe there is.

Hope does give us focus and purpose. It's how we get things done. Anger can also inspire action. There's nothing like fury to address an injustice. Anger, though, has a tendency to align itself with pride, resentment, envy, and several other less-attractive emotions. A realistic version of hope seems to be necessary to forward motion, to progress, perhaps even to our survival. Such a version will need refinement. It can't be predicated on guarantees. Neither masters of the universe nor a universal master can assure a favorable outcome each and every time.

We're asking a lot from this hope.

While hope therapy has been used to treat depression, it's more challenging to imagine it working on skepticism. It's actually logical to feel awful about the human condition nowadays. A skeptic might be forgiven for wondering if hope can have a relationship to a practical, clear-headed, reason-based living. Yet we all yearn for meaning. While that feeling may not be wholly reasonable or strictly logical, it means something.

I based my previous book, *Because I Say So,* on my experiences as a 9/11 widow. I ended it with a suggestion that hope has value. To be perfectly honest, I don't know whether I believed that or I simply wanted to believe it.

While I never thought my loss provided me with any special status, moral or otherwise, I gained some insight into traumatic loss. My concern was with whether and how I might be able to recover, to the extent possible. I wondered whether some sort of realistic hope could or should or had to play a part in that recovery, even in small doses.

Realistic hope is gaining currency in some quarters. I was pleased to run across an article appearing in *The Harvard Review* entitled "Hope is a Strategy (Well, Sort Of)." In it, the author, Deborah Mills-Scofield, notes that "hope is a critical part of achieving a strategy when based on what is possible; perhaps not highly probable, but possible." She also says, "Hope recognizes the reality that failure happens, success is not assured, the laws of physics don't change and prudence is needed to discern when to persevere—and when to pivot." [6]

Practical hope as a business model: I like it.

My mission is more modest and certainly more personal: to see whether some sort of, let's call it, managed hope can be a driver in my life (and the lives of any others interested in trying it), and what form it might take. The notion of hope in small doses may seem unnecessarily cautious, but that's pretty much how I roll. I'm working with who I am. Besides, I might as well start small; I can always ask for seconds.

Asking questions seems a natural way to arrive at answers. Here are a few that occurred to me, some of which I've already begun to address:

1. What is hope?
2. Are there different kinds of hope?
3. Is hope good or bad—or both?
4. Who has hope and who doesn't?
5. What is the relationship of hope to well-being?
6. What happens when we lose hope?
7. How is hope related to meaning or purpose?
8. Is hope necessary?

That's barely scratching the surface, I expect. Maybe what I really want to know is: What form of hope might enhance my life and the lives of people I know may be curious, cautious, care-worn, or who are concerned about being disappointed or appearing foolish? What kind of hope might be universally acceptable or, even better, universally beneficial?

Contemplating various forms of hope might seem a luxury unavailable to many. Out in the world are men, women, and children trying to figure out where their next meals are coming from. I'm not about to tell anyone in such a position, or anyone struggling with illness or depravation that they need to buck up, think good thoughts, stay the course, etc. It's pretty obvious that positive thinking has its limitations.

Hope doesn't by itself feed a family or heal a sick child. I'm not yet sure hope can override the cumulative effect of life's negative experiences, from the tragic to the annoying. Aren't we all likely to encounter setbacks? What are we supposed to be learning from our missteps and mistakes and even from the colossal unfairness of life? Where does hope factor into the moment, when you've been at the top of the mountain and you find yourself plummeting down the other side? How does hope relate to endurance? Questions and more questions.

Mortality is on my radar these days. There's the death of my husband, followed in quick succession by the death of one parent after another. Losing loved ones in such a concentrated period of time knocked me clear out of whatever comfort zone I thought I inhabited. More years of life are behind me than ahead of me, unless I turn out to be a freak of nature; and I'm not sure I want to be. Pain, mostly irritating but occasionally debilitating, has become a regular visitor in my body. On certain days, I'm unlikely to entertain any illusions of a pleasant future, whether it's five minutes or fifteen years away. I don't even want to *think* about hope, much less write about it. I wonder then, how do people without resources, without freedom, with additional burdens of family or illness or so many other obstacles—how do these people cope emotionally? Many impoverished people turn out to be deeply religious. Some belief systems both offer explanations and promises in the form of future reward. But religion simply isn't the answer for plenty of others trying to navigate the reality of chance, circumstance, and unpredictability. What might work for any of us?

When it comes to life as we know it (or don't know it), I always end up with more questions than answers. I think many people do. We'd all like to figure out how to live fully and enjoyably, but not all of us can console ourselves with the certainty that everything will be taken care of. Sometimes we can find models in ordinary people living what we might believe are extraordinary lives. Later on, I'll have something to say about a young woman with a devastating disease who is impressively resolute. Meanwhile, let me turn my attention to one of my role models, the great physicist and cosmologist, Stephen Hawking.

Dr. Hawking, who has suffered from a form of amyotrophic lateral sclerosis (ALS) for nearly fifty years, directs research at the Center for Theoretical Cosmology in London. He may be the longest-living patient with the disease. He's lived his entire life with limitations (except to his fantastic mind) and in proximity to death. He uses a customized wheelchair and speaks by way of a computerized voice simulator and a cheek muscle that allows him to select the words he wants to use. Answers to questions take days for him to put together and the very thought that he's written many important books and papers is mind-boggling.

In 2011, Dr. Hawking gave an interview to a *New York Times* reporter, following a speech at Arizona State University called, "My Brief Life." Per standard protocol, he had prerecorded most of his responses based on questions submitted in advance. He chose to sit with the reporter while the responses were played back. The reporter came up with an impromptu question, however, about Dr. Hawking's university presentation, about why it was so personal—a question he willingly, if painstakingly, answered, letter by letter, word by word, over a five-minute interlude: "I hope my experience will help other people."[7]

With much humility, I would like to borrow Dr. Hawking's response to offer as explanation the reason for this book and what I look forward to sharing what I've learned about the benefits—the joys, actually—of hope in small doses.

Notes

1 AP Stylebook.
2 Cole, "Correlations."
3 Sahgal, "Conquering Fear."
4 Ehrenreich, "Overrated Optimism."
5 Colihan, "Hope Therapy."
6 Mills-Scofield "Hope is a Strategy."
7 Dreifus, "Life."

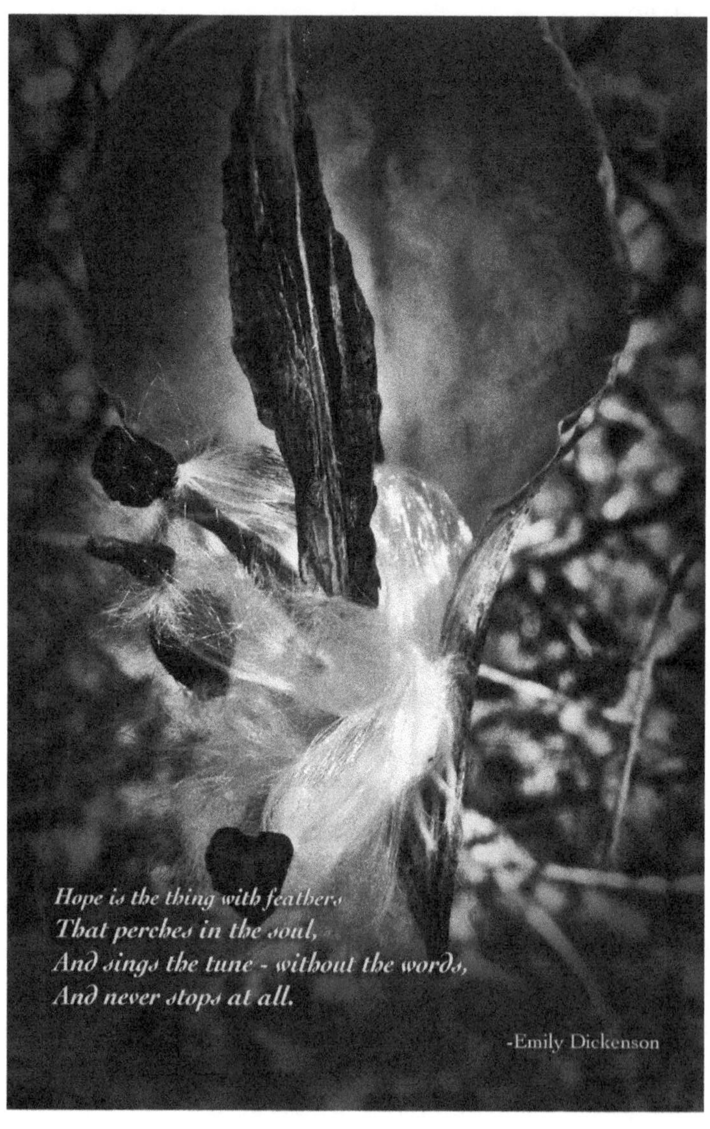
Hope is the thing with feathers
That perches in the soul,
And sings the tune - without the words,
And never stops at all.
-Emily Dickenson

CHAPTER 2

The Thing with Feathers

Hope is the dream of a waking man.
–Aristotle

I'm a sucker for definitions. I want to make sure all the participants in any discussion are on the same page. It's dangerous to assume we all share the same idea about what something means. For instance, after my husband was killed on 9/11, I began to hear the phrase "moral authority", as in "the moral authority of the families" or "the moral authority of the United States." I wondered what people meant—or thought they meant. When I began my research, however, I found very little that defined or attempted to explain *moral authority*. Eventually, I began to understand the phrase as granting a free pass. That's why *Because I Say So* is subtitled *Moral Authority's Dangerous Appeal.*

Hope, on the other hand, has no shortage of definitions. The problem may be that it has too many.

The evolutionary psychologist, Robert Plutchik, introduced his theory of adaptive human emotional responses using a color wheel[1] to illustrate the eight primary and eight secondary emotions. He identifies *ecstasy, admiration, terror, amazement, grief, loathing, rage* and *vigilance* as primary emotions and lists *joy, trust, fear, surprise, sadness, disgust, anger* and *anticipation* as neighboring (and slightly more complex) secondary emotional responses. A third category is also included. Hope is nowhere to be found.

So what? Anticipation is there; and that's the same as hope, isn't it? No, it isn't. *Anticipation* is the brain's failsafe system by which it gets the body ready for what happens next, good or bad. In a later chapter, I'll take a look at what the neuroscientists see when they look at the brain under the influence of various emotions. One thing that's clear, however, is that hope is a complex state that involves both emotion and cognition. Hope can make you feel happy or look forward to something, but it's not instinctive.

What about optimism? Positive psychology websites seem to use optimism and hope interchangeably, even though optimism represents a more generalized outlook. Certainly being hopeful could make us *feel* optimistic. Optimistic people are more likely to embrace hope.

Hope, however, is *not* the same as optimism. We can take the word of psychologists like C.R Snyder. A leading cognitive therapist, he distinguished between optimism and hope, concluding the latter is a belief that could be learned. Even Václav Havel, playwright and former president of the Czech Republic, insisted on the difference. In *Disturbing the Peace*, he noted: "Hope is definitely not the same thing as optimism. It is not the conviction that something will turn out well, but the certainty that something makes sense, regardless of how it turns out."[2] The certainty doesn't concern the outcome, by the way, but the correctness of pursuing the action.

The very complexity of hope is what makes it teachable, Snyder believed. It's not something that simply *occurs*. Patients can be taught to hope, to apply it to problem solving. They can learn to set realistic goals, develop a plan of action, and create acceptable alternatives in order to retain flexibility and not lose the feeling of hope. Snyder suggested chronic or seriously depressed patients must be taught to hope as a part of any successful treatment. The application of hope (the belief) could conceivably generate feelings of optimism (the emotion).

Snyder defines hope as "The sum of the mental willpower and waypower you have for your goals."[3] In order to understand what he's talking about, one would have to read his book, *The Psychology of Hope: You Can Get There from Here*. Snyder presents a veritable instruction manual on how to teach and learn hope, and it's interesting and informative enough to deserve a closer look. I'll get to that in Chapter 5, if you're a jumping-ahead sort. Anyway, a part of me admires the efforts to develop a methodology that can help us acquire the appropriate mindset; but seriously, is that how most of us think about hope?

I searched traditional dictionary sites to see how linguists handled hope, the noun. There was some consistency across three sites. *Merriam-Webster* called it "desire accompanied by expectation of or belief in fulfillment";[4] *Oxford* defined it as "a belief that something you want will happen";[5] and the *Free Dictionary* identified it as "the feeling that what is wanted can be had or that events will turn out for the best."[6]

These definitions are widely accepted, but they still give me problems. In all of them I see what I call "the expectation clause." So many ideas about what hope does, or means, seem to get derailed when burdened with ideas about what *ought* to be a particular outcome.

The Internet is a treasure trove of views on hope, at least on those sites where someone is selling a book, promoting a methodology, or simply making an observation. These custom-tailored descriptions of hope support various approaches. At a site called The Difference Between, hope is contrasted with faith as follows: "Hope is an action predicated on uncertainty...[It] is more logically based, as it recognizes the facts, and simply desires that those facts add up to a positive outcome..."[7] The author goes on to define faith as more spiritual and more certain. He or she also calls faith a "psychosis" and hope a fact-based projection, so there is clearly some bias at work.

One definition of hope I found initially persuasive is offered on the website of an organization called Changing Minds. I like the idea of being able to change someone's mind whose thinking is "stuck" (in my view, of course) without resorting to threats or coercion. Changing Minds claims to be the "largest...in the world on all aspects of how we change what others think, believe, feel and do."[8] The requisite book is advertised, along with a plea to vote in a contest for the year's Top Sales and Marketing Resource Site. Changing Minds even has a sister site, Creative Minds, which offers tools in marketing and presentation.

Both the site and the group behind it appear to be part of an ambitious project belonging to one David Straker. He's listed as an adjunct assistant clinical professor of psychiatry at Columbia University Medical Center, and an assistant clinical professor of psychiatry at Albert Einstein College. His definition of hope is "expectation moderated by probabilistic estimation of a desired event."[9] I'm not entirely sure what he means, but his site includes a curve that undulates between utter certainty and absolute despair. Presumably, the curve represents the spectrum along which, as near as I can tell, we might locate a reasonable or "managed" version of hope.

Changing Minds and its affiliates are marketing sites. They offer a spin on hope that suggests it can be bottled and sold. This isn't a novel approach; it's the essence of most advertising. Charles Revson, the founder of the Revlon cosmetics company, famously remarked about its products, "In the factory we make cosmetics; in the drugstore we sell hope."[10] Decades earlier, the radio personality, Helen Landon Cass, gave this advice to a group of conventioneers: "Hope is whatever you're selling, standing in for whatever the customer might desire. Sell them their dreams. Sell them what they longed for and hoped for. Sell them this hope and you won't have to worry about selling the goods."[11]

Straker's observations, if they can be separated from their consumer orientation, are worth considering. If a marketing model begins with hope as an "expectation moderated by probabilistic estimation of a desired event," then managing or, yes, manipulating hope so that it moves to a more optimistic state is how we change minds...or sell products.

Okay, I admit it; teaching, encouraging, or "managing" hope for the purpose of marketing makes me queasy.

Looking further:

On another website, the author of an article entitled "What is hope?" defines it as "the belief that circumstances in the future will be better."[12] She goes on to state, "[Hope] is not a wish that things will get better, but an actual belief, even when there may be no evidence that anything will change."[13] The distinction between hoping and wishing is apparently crucial. According to definitions provided by instructors on an ESL (English as a second language) forum, to hope is to suggest a more likely or specific outcome than to wish, which is some sort of vague desire. I spent a little time reading the answers given to the confused student. I can understand why non-English speakers have so much trouble learning the language; native speakers don't even agree on the meaning of *wish, desire, expectation,* or *hope.*

Certain religions define hope quite explicitly. The Catholic Encyclopedia says of hope that it is a "Divine virtue by which we confidently expect, with God's help, to reach eternal felicity as well as to have at our disposal the means of securing it."[14] Furthermore, hope, at least in Catholic theology, is "an infused virtue...directly implanted in the soul by Almighty God." It's also a duty that can be destroyed only by "the sin of despair."[15]

No equivocating there.

The secular forms of hope include versions that are both me-centric (if I believe I can make it happen, then I can make it happen) and we-centric (we can work together to make this happen). In most cases, hope still ties itself to certainty that something will occur as a result either of a higher power or the power of our minds.

As a working skeptic (I'm actually working to moderate my skepticism with some flags-in-the-ground convictions), I'm open to faith in principle, especially faith that is divorced from the requirement that it be of the religious variety. Conveniently, a number of philosophers have already tackled the subject. Susan Neiman, whose views on moral clarity provide answers for both believers and non-theists, proposes faith in the notion of progress. Steven Pinker suggests we have faith in our own moral evolution.

Pinker, in his book, *The Better Angels of Our Nature,* presents an impressive amount of data to support his thesis that violence is declining. His larger argument—that this decline demonstrates we're becoming more tolerant, reasonable, and kindly creatures—appears to be at odds with current attitudes about our present condition. The rise of extremist groups abroad, the spread of economic calamity, the air of despair and fractiousness that inform our political discourse indicate that we're not improving at all, according to many. They let Pinker and his publisher know it.

In addition to predictable criticism from both the scientific and psychological communities, there were many contributions from commenters who reacted viscerally to reviews of Pinker's book (in some cases, it appears, without having tackled any part of the 800-plus page book itself). They seemed infuriated with the notion that our species might be getting nicer. Pinker and his supporters were accused of being hopelessly naïve or dangerously deluded, cut off from reality and blind to circumstances. The protesters said Pinker had failed to recognize a new kind of economic and psychological cruelty ("Preying upon the weak has changed from cutting off noses to holding people's welfare in one's hands," noted one contrarian).[16] They accused him of ignoring the calculation that goes into waging the more impersonal forms of warfare—those fought with "smart" bombs and lethal pathogens. Others charged Pinker with willfully ignoring events that might contradict his argument, such as genocide throughout Africa.

Pinker's methodology is fair game, as is his research; although the latter seems comprehensive and the former perfectly valid as a psycho-scientific premise. The tone of the comments led me to wonder if the commenters were appalled by the suggestion that humans were evolving. That saddens more than surprises me. I liked Pinker's book, parts of which I read completely, and parts of which I admittedly skimmed. I've always thought we'd eventually discover the advantages of being nice to one another. Then again, I don't think we live in the worst of times.

Many people apparently do. Journalists and pollsters used words like "demoralized" or "frightened" to describe the current mood in the United States. In the spring of 2011, Gallup conducted a survey about American's vision of the future. Fewer than half of those adults polled believed the standard of living would improve for the next generation. [17] The general malaise extends beyond the United States. The global division of Pew Research found in an early 2015 poll that younger people in Europe were not feeling particularly optimistic about anything.[18] Polls like these, which demonstrate widespread dissatisfaction with politics, economics, environment, or quality of life in general seem to indicate that at least for the foreseeable future, our expectations have been muted.

Again, I'm not surprised. Financial hard times and social upheaval are likely to bring everyone down and the way forward is unclear. We're being told our aspirations and expectations need to be "reasonable." Insofar as that advice seems to be a reversal of the mantra that we could "have it all," it's a bitter pill to swallow. We presumably know we really can't have all of whatever it is we're seeking; it's just difficult to absorb the new message while being hit with examples of easy wealth and conspicuous consumption all around. Well, no one said life was fair.

Does hope then become irrelevant? Are we suggesting it has no place in our world? Would we ask hope to take a hike, maybe hide out until things get better? How are we to navigate an unpredictable world, where neither man nor divine entity can be counted on to make things better in any given moment (or decade or generation)? What kind of attitude can we adopt that doesn't recommend we capitulate to a grim and fruitless existence?

Humanists, who for years have been trying to craft an optimistic human-centric message, have moved toward a more neutral look at life on earth. Michael Werner, past president of the American Humanist Association, observed in an essay for *The Humanist* that we secular types fully understand human nature has potential for both good and evil. We can't know at any given time who will choose which path and how influential he or she, or they, will be. Nevertheless, we must forge ahead, even in the presence of doubt; because we don't really have any other reasonable choice. Life in the face of that tepid endorsement seems very bleak indeed.

At least Werner ended on a slightly more optimistic note in which he acknowledged our propensity to "long for an evocative whole story and higher vision that lifts our hearts and ennobles our lives."[19] That's still a bit more passive than I'd like my hope to be. Longing is good, but it leaves me wanting. Suddenly we've moved over to hope in really, really small doses, which doesn't provide much in the way of motivation. Does hope really need to be so constrained?

Depends on how broad your brush is.

Michael Meade is the founder of the Mosaic Multicultural Foundation, "a network of artists, healers, social activists, and community builders" seeking to "encourage greater understanding between people with diverse and divergent backgrounds and experiences." In a piece he wrote on his *Huffington Post* blog, Meade introduced the idea of two levels of hope. One is based on outsized and unrealistic expectations (the "wrong" kind); the second grows out of disappointment and is thus richer and more informative. One might simply characterize Meade as a New Age spiritualist, but his view looks outward as well as within. I found myself pulled into his writing, eager to learn whether his "level two" hope might work for the dubious and the doubtful.

Meade tells us, "Most hopes turn out to be false hopes based upon wishful thinking and false expectations that cannot survive encounters with harsh reality. The problem isn't simply that people lose hope, but that hope turns into its opposite: despair."[20]

Meade reassures us despair is not a dead end ("it is the nature of hope to become lost," he notes), but a darkness from which we can access the version of hope that's found "not by clinging to old dreams or by denying despair, but by surviving it."

What's missing when we feel hopeless, he continues, is "genuine imagination." We can get through the bad times by "connecting to the underlying spirit of life and the hidden resiliency of the individual soul [that] is the source of genuine hope."[21]

That's as inspirational as it gets, a variation on the theme that the darkest hour is just before dawn. Understanding how to reach deeper hope, however, is not as obvious. Most definitions of hope include some sort of expectation about what will come to pass. Meade suggests that's precisely what trips us up. Really? Are we to set goals without assuming a favorable outcome? Are we supposed to go after what we want without expecting we'll get it?

We are. The hope Meade proposes is an all-purpose state of mind, an umbrella of sorts, willfully generalized. It requires that we embrace the idea of hopefulness without attaching ourselves to a specific result, without even knowing whether we'll succeed at any given task. This hope is in the nature of a belief that something good *could* result from an effort or a set of goals. There are no assurances except those which come from belief in the human spirit.

"Level two" hope won't appeal to everyone. We might prefer a version in which guarantees are made, either by a divine entity or by the assumption that each of us will surely achieve whatever it is we set our minds to. Those versions of hope require certainty, and certainty isn't what we get in this life. Meade's hope thrives and expands on being less than certain.

I've been told hope is too "risky," at least the kind that requires an acceptance of uncertainty. Yet uncertainty means possibility, and possibility is what sets free our imaginations.

Janet Asimov, wife of the late science fiction writer, was addressing uncertainty when she wrote in *Humanist Network News*, "I like to believe...I've accepted uncertainty about almost everything, while yearning to believe that apples and bookstores and Lincoln Center won't go extinct."[22]

Would her meaning have been different if she'd used *hoping* instead of *yearning*? Would *hoping* imply she was actively seeking a way to make sure Lincoln Center survived and apples continued to grow? Or is hope inexorably tied to vague aspirational longing? I asked a few friends, smart serious people at various stages in their lives, to define hope. Their spontaneous responses displayed neither irrationality nor unfulfilled desire. They weren't pinned to either a particular outcome, nor a general expectation. Instead they were uplifting, imaginative, and very nearly ethereal.

For me, hope has been and will always be a "pilot light"—it stays on and fuels my inner core. —Joan

I think hope is transcendent. It's not the light at the end of

the tunnel, but what's beyond the light. —Ken

Hope is necessary to the continuation of seeking perfection in creativity. Hope provides us with a positive mind image...over which we really have total control, regardless of mitigating factors. —Gary

It's the eternal four-year-old in us. —Matt

These definitions are deeply personal; they're also imprecise. Maybe that's the point. Hope, being a mixture of conscious belief and subconscious emotion, is hard to pin down. It can manifest as irrational, calming, exuberant, delusional, or therapeutic. Even if it's a belief system, it's still subject to mood swings. Is there a practical version of hope that works in tandem with the more positive emotions we all want in our lives, like happiness, joy, or optimism? Is that even possible?

Notes

1 Plutchik, "Emotions and Life."
2 Havel, *Disturbing the Peace*, 181.
3 Snyder, *The Psychology of Hope*, 5.
4 "Hope," *Merriam-Webster*.
5 "Hope," *Oxford Learners Dictionary*.
6 "Hope," *Free Dictionary*.
7 "Difference Between Hope and Faith."
8 "Changing Minds."
9 Ibid.
10 Brainyquote.com, "Revson."
11 Feigenbaum, "1920s."
12 Edmonds, "What is Hope."
13 Ibid.

14 "Hope," *The Catholic Encyclopedia.*
15 Ibid.
16 Zimmer, "Human Nature's Pathologist."
17 Mendez, "Optimism."
18 Stokes, "Europe's Kids are Moody and Depressed."
19 Werner, "Humanism 101."
20 Meade, "Hidden Hope."
21 Ibid.
22 Asimov, "Accepting Uncertainty."

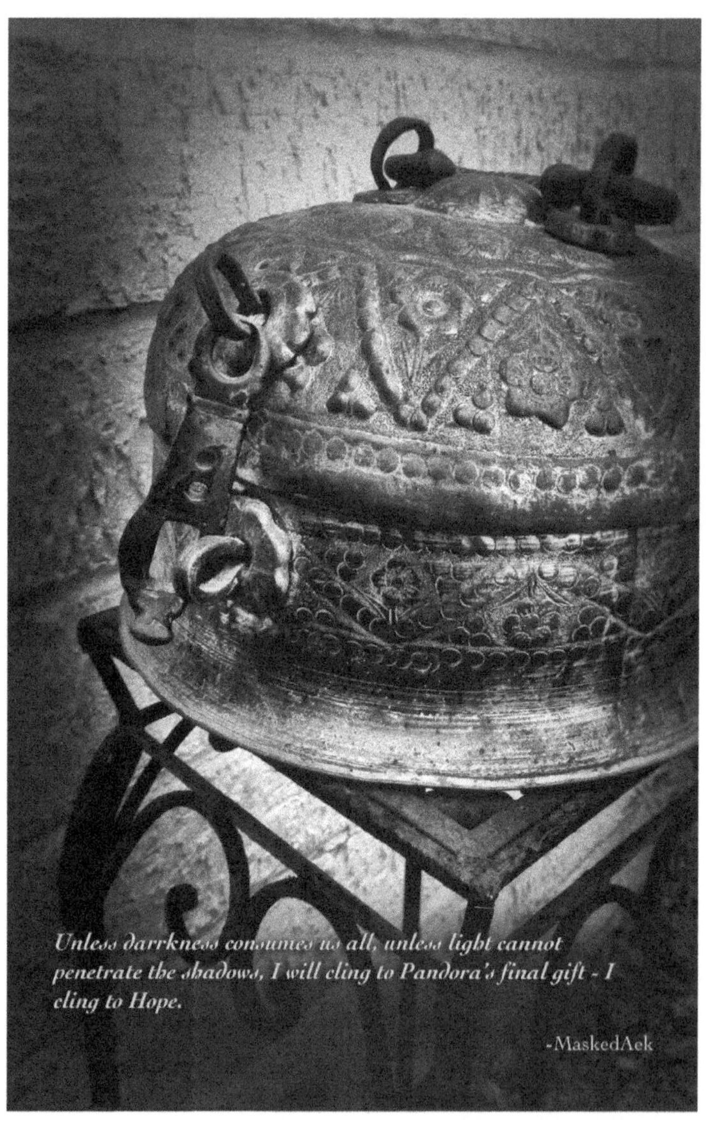
Unless darrkness consumes us all, unless light cannot penetrate the shadows, I will cling to Pandora's final gift - I cling to Hope.
-MaskedAek

CHAPTER 3

PANDORA'S MISTAKE

Only Hope was left within her unbreakable house, she remained under the lip of the jar, and did not fly away. Before [it could], Pandora replaced the lid of the jar. This was the will of aegis-bearing Zeus the Cloudgatherer.

–Hesiod

Poor Pandora! She's to blame for the world's ills, at least as Greek mythology tells it. According to the most familiar version of the story, by the seventh-century BCE poet, Hesiod, Pandora was made by the gods as the first woman. By all accounts she was beautiful; some described her as cunning and most certainly vain. The gods had their own agendas. They plied lovely Pandora with presents and gave her various abilities. Zeus was harboring revenge fantasies against mankind because Prometheus had earlier stolen fire from him. His gift was contrived to be deliberately troublesome, both a warning to his mortal subjects and a test of his newest creation's ability to obey. Pandora's Box (actually a jar in the original Greek, which figures in some interpretations of the tale) contained a litany of the world's future evils—hate, pain, selfishness, vengefulness, deceitfulness, and destructiveness. Some stories also throw in sickness and starvation, as those were certainly in abundance in ancient times. The container came with orders NOT to open it.

Whether Pandora opened the gift out of curiosity or disobedience is subject to debate, but the outcome was the same. All manner of trouble descended on what had been a perfect existence for mankind. To make things worse, Pandora supposedly closed the lid before hope managed to escape, making her guilty of bad judgment as well as insubordination.

If the story is merely about obedience to one's maker, Pandora certainly failed. The gods were counting on her weakness (or deceit), which suggests they didn't have the best interests of humankind at heart. Greek gods weren't known for their beneficence. They often behaved like spoiled children or nasty despots, albeit with superpowers. Pandora also proved to be a helpful scapegoat. She unleashed, not for the last time, the enduring cultural conceit that women were to blame for many, if not all, of man's troubles, inspiring misogynists for years to come.

Pandora's actions were more than a cautionary tale. They were a way of explaining the inherent inequality, unfairness, and uncertainty of the world in which ancient mankind lived. Life was hard; there was no salvation, nor was there much in the way of comfort. Whether hope stayed in the box or left last, nothing could displace the ills that had found a permanent home among the living.

Many well-known Greeks believed fate was preordained. Hope was useless at best and, to some, as evil as its companions who escaped Pandora's container. Hesiod, in his *Works and Days*, observed, "The idle man who waits on empty hope...lays to heart mischief-making..."[1] As the presumed author of the story of Pandora, he presents a view of hope as troublemaker. When asked to explain what he thought hope to be, Aristotle is reputed to have said, "The dream of a waking man."[2] The dramatist Euripides had one of his characters in *Iphigenia in Tauris* remark, "That glittering hope is immemorial and beckons many men to their undoing."[3]

The view of hope as a useless and often cruel mental state has been a recurring theme among disaffected writers throughout history. Shakespeare wrote in *The Rape of Lucrece*, "And so by hoping more, they have but lesse."[4] Ben Franklin, writing as Poor Richard in his almanac by that name, observed, "He that lives upon hope will die fasting."[5] Friedrich Nietzsche no doubt enhanced his reputation for blunt bleakness when he wrote, "In truth [hope] is the most evil of evils, for it prolongs man's torment."[6] Nietzsche, author of other memorable quotes such as "God is dead," was particularly scornful of religion's promises of afterlife rewards.

The writers above were unlikely to have turned to religion as an antidote to life's many miseries since early religion wasn't much comfort. The disciples were likely to mete out punishments in the name of their deity, whose harshness blocked out any imagined rewards. While some sects continue to practice rough justice, modern religion emphasizes a hope that seeks to smooth over life's unfairness.

Western religion in particular elevates the sort of hope that thrives in the face of adversity, turning it into a virtue. We're not talking about Meade's second level of hope. This hope is viewed as both courageous and audacious in its unwavering conviction that a supreme being will provide. The title of Barack Obama's book, *The Audacity of Hope*, was inspired, he admitted, by a sermon given by his then-pastor Jeremiah Wright. Many portions of the sermon have been taken out of context to make various points about Obama's policies, etc. What interests me is how the sermon riffed off a parable about a painting of a woman with a harp. In the picture, the instrument she holds has only one string and the woman is ragged and apparently wounded. Instead of bemoaning her fate or wishing things were different, the woman sings God's praises, we are told. She is courageous in choosing to hope despite her wretched circumstances. Her audacity is in holding to her absolute certainty in a divine plan despite her difficulties.

That conclusion doesn't represent either audacity or hope for many of us. In fact, it's much more audacious to embrace hope in conjunction with a goal but without the promise of eternal life or divine reward. Daring to hope, judging this life worthy of that hope—now that's something to sing about.

So much is out of our control. We're confronted not only with our own thwarted desires, but with an unpredictable setting. Little can be counted on. Worse, the bad often appears to overwhelm the good. Children are kidnapped or killed; illness makes random claims on the best and brightest among us; poverty grinds many into the ground; hatred abounds. Hope seems to be at the bottom of the scrimmage dominated by the world's ills. How can we possibly invest in a belief so outmatched, so lacking in potency that it might just as well be crouching in an ancient container? Even the expression "hope against hope" suggests not so much courage as a fool's errand, a hope without a benefactor or a reward. Is it any wonder that those of us who can't sing the praises of an unseen deity feel condemned to wander around wrapped in a metaphorical blanket of gloom?

That was pretty much where things stood for me as a high school freshman. Hope was all eager needs, unreachable dreams, big disappointments, and real fears about the world I was living in. No doubt hormonal surges and roller-coaster emotions played their parts, combined with a view of myself as "alienated"—awkward, smart, poor at sports, and worse at belonging. My transitional years also took place against a backdrop of tumultuous events. President Kennedy had just been assassinated, the South was engulfed in racial unrest, and the United States was poised to enter a war in Southeast Asia. While I was still an infant, my state senator, Joe McCarthy, went on a Communist witch-hunt; and while I was in grade school, my hometown featured a serial killer and body snatcher named Ed Gein. In sixth grade, we crouched under wooden desks in anticipation of a nuclear attack; my neighbors were building fallout shelters.

I knew my upbringing was advantaged and my life relatively stable. I'd also learned anyone's life could be up-ended at any time. My grandparents had come to the United States to escape persecution. Some of their cousins had been shot alongside mass graves they were forced to dig for them-selves before they were killed. My father had been part of the liberation army entering Auschwitz; we stayed up one night talking about *The Diary of Ann Frank*. The United States had interned Japanese- American citizens not a decade be-fore I was born. No wonder the entire enterprise of living seemed to be so uncertain.

I absorbed the works of early twentieth-century Amer-ican writers like Ambrose Bierce and John dos Passos. Irony and satire appealed to me; I adored Kurt Vonnegut. I was es-pecially enamored of the French philosophers like Jean-Paul Sartre and Albert Camus. Sartre was well known as a philos-opher and, later on, a political activist and Marxist. An avowed atheist, he recognized the uncertainty of existence. Yet Sartre didn't believe (as is mistakenly assumed) that ex-istentialism was an invitation to live one's life in hopelessness and despair. In an important speech he gave in 1946, he set out to refute the charges that his philosophy focused on the more sordid aspects of human existence. In fact, he observed, what frightened his critics was that his doctrine "confronts man with a possibility of choice."[7]

"Man is nothing else but that which he makes of himself. That is the first principle of existentialism...The first effect of existentialism is that it puts every man in possession of himself as he is, and places the entire responsibility for his existence squarely upon his own shoulders. And, when we say that man is responsible for himself, we do not mean that he is responsible only for his own individuality, but that he is responsible for all men."[8]

Sartre identifies our angst as related to our commitment to make mankind into the best possible version of itself. "Man is condemned to live free,"[9] he asserts. I guess that's not a happy thought for some. We've got all this freedom and no one to tell us what choices to make. What do we do with it? Maybe the key is to keep the weight off your shoulders, cut yourself a break every now and then. I wonder if Sartre had a sense of humor.

I digress.

Sartre tackles the argument that existentialism is atheism, saying, "Existentialism is not atheist in the sense that it would exhaust itself in demonstrations of the nonexistence of God. It declares, rather, that even if God existed, that would make no difference from its point of view. Not that we believe God does exist, but we think that the real problem is not that of his existence; what man needs is to find himself again and to understand that nothing can save him from himself, not even a valid proof of the existence of God. In this sense, existentialism is optimistic. It is a doctrine of action, and it is only by self-deception, by confining their own despair with ours, that Christians can describe us as without hope."[10]

I hadn't remembered this speech from high school. Or maybe I did and focused on the part that says we have to save ourselves. Perhaps I missed the point that we *can* save ourselves by taking action instead of counting on help from above. Maybe I assumed existentialism stopped at despair rather than pushing toward possibility. Sartre wasn't all doom and gloom. He didn't assume that we live in the best of all possible worlds or that God always makes it right. But he did think people could make a positive impact in the world by working towards the best possible outcome. Many religious leaders have always insisted and continue to insist existentialists, atheists, non-theists, and agnostics can't experience hope because, in their view, "a world without God is a world without hope."[11] But isn't the idea that we can make things better a hopeful idea? I think it is.

Sadly, Sartre is little understood as a proponent of secular hope. Instead, he became embroiled in a tempest about whether or not he had embraced a redemptive, religious version of hope near the end of his life. This change of heart was presumably indicated by a series of interviews he did in 1980. But Ronald Aronson, a noted Sartre biographer, suggests in an introduction to the most recent translation of the book that Sartre was simply engaged in musing about morality and mortality, reviewing and refining his ideas about the social contract at the end of his life.[12]

Rereading Sartre and especially the criticisms he encountered, I'm struck by how easily prevailing mindsets cubbyhole errant or nontraditional ideas. Sartre and his contemporary Camus were giants of philosophy in their day and popular study subjects when I was young. Still, the view I got as an American student was anything but nuanced, even though I was taught by young women with their own romanticized notions of alienation. Sartre and Camus were atheists; they wrote about the starkness, the hopelessness of the human condition, end of story.

Or was it?

Albert Camus grew up in Algeria in impoverished conditions. His father was killed early in World War I during the Battle of the Marne and he was raised by his deaf mother. Camus worked hard to obtain a scholarship in order to continue his education, but a long bout of tuberculosis and constant money worries required him to cut back on his studies while working. During World War II, Camus edited an underground resistance paper.

Camus' writing was influenced by poverty and illness and by the wartime atrocities he witnessed. He questioned the meaning of human existence in most of his work and was great friends with Sartre until a late-in-life quarrel. Still, he rejected the label of existentialism, declaring in one interview, "No, I am not an existentialist. Sartre and I are always surprised to see our names linked."[13] He was also associated with absurdism, but preferred being seen as a champion of individualism.

Camus' *The Plague* describes a town faced with bubonic plague that must be quarantined. The doctor and his cohorts struggle to save lives while recognizing the impossibility of their task. Characters become attached to other characters, at least one of whom will die. Perhaps this is worth nothing more than a shoulder shrug in the current environment of young adult books like *The Hunger Games*. People die: good people, young people. Life is absurd.

Camus doesn't throw up his hands at death; instead, he shakes his fist at it. He puts his characters in an untenable situation and has them gradually awaken to their own helplessness, but he doesn't let them give up. They act responsibly, even nobly, bonding over their shared sense of duty. Camus finds decency in a human spirit that survives and thrives in the face of adversity. His characters are resilient; they don't endlessly despair. There's really no time and no point to it. They connect to one another, they challenge the odds, and they work at saving whatever lives they can. The book is life-affirming, evidence of a philosophy Camus expanded in later works.

The American poet Emily Dickinson lived in near seclusion with her parents. Never married, she connected with others through a prolific amount of correspondence replete with thoughts, concerns, and odd bits of poetry. Dickinson's writing suggests she was obsessed with death. At the same time, she sought to make peace with mortality and to find serenity. In her famous poem, "Hope is a Thing with Feathers," she observes the bird singing in bad weather as well as good, despite sometimes harsh conditions, and notwithstanding it doesn't "know" the words to its song. Because the bird is doing what makes it happy—singing—it's able to bring comfort and happiness to other creatures.

Realistically, we presume the bird is simply obeying a biological imperative. As for giving us comfort, birds aren't any more inclined to think about our welfare than were the Greek gods. However, Dickinson's bird is a potent representation of hope, as are both Camus' resilient human spirit and Sartre's call for responsibility and action.

If these three, whose writing tended to highlight the fragility of life, still managed to seek hope in the observable world, why is it so difficult for the rest of us? Humanists focus on belief in humankind. With optimism tempered by experience, they point to our *potential* to take action in order to improve the human condition. For those who don't see value in resilience or in a bird's song, the world may appear either depressing or simply random. They might sink into depression or affect ennui, rejecting hope in any form as a futile or even dangerous delusion.

All these approaches are nothing more than accommodations to the single unvarying truth about the human condition: we're mortal. Personally, I have nothing against accommodation, as long as it comes to rest somewhere south of denial and north of resignation. As to those who insist hope has no place in their lives, I'm curious about whether they've truly landed in a sweet spot they might call clear-eyed acceptance.

My friend Doug swears he lives without experiencing hope and assures me he finds contentment simply by living in the present. As he explains it, he takes precautions and makes preparations, but doesn't try to summon an emotional state of mind that might mean disappointment. That's what hope is to him. "Why open myself up to that?" he asks. No hope, no bother, he says and promises he's not a bit unhappy. Doug does some meditation. He leans toward Eastern philosophies that don't make a grand distinction between the divine and the secular. He thinks nature unfolds as it is meant to unfold and, like some Buddhists, he is able to enjoy what is without thinking about what will be.

I find it hard to argue with the idea of "being in the moment." It has certain advantages; if you're experiencing an unpleasant or difficult flash, wait it out. Another will come along...momentarily. But aren't Buddhists actively involved in seeking hope via immortality: first enlightenment, then further evolution through reincarnation, and eventually, nirvana? Is Doug conveniently leaving out that part?

Michael Meade, the Mosaic founder, goes back to the Pandora myth to show how it might apply to an earthbound sort of hope. He makes the case for a version of Pandora's story that doesn't fault her for all the troubles on earth. Pandora, he points out, was also called *Anesidora* ("she who sends up gifts"), a title she shares with even older earth goddesses in mythology. She is, he concludes, the spirit of earth, a giver of gifts, and a source of both life that has passed and new life. He reminds us that Hesiod's Pandora had a jar, not a box; the jar in those days was used for preserving certain foodstuffs but also to hold funeral ashes.

"I am connecting the sense of the living earth from which life continually renews itself with the image of a hidden hope grounded in a deeper understanding of life on earth," Meade explains at one point in his analysis.[14] Cynics (and I've been a member of that group on occasion) may roll their eyes at the New Age-sounding language. Personally, I like where he's going. Pandora as a symbol of Earth Mother has been lost, he suggests, to the more popular idea that Woman released into the world a box full of sorrow and pain. I'm sure I'm not the only woman who'd like to return to Meade's suggested version of the story.

I don't know if Pandora's reputation can be redeemed. She may have been, as we've heard, the creation of a capricious, narcissistic, and vengeful deity. Whether she released hope too late or left it to cower, it exists in our world. Hope is a powerful force, capable of blinding or inspiring us, depending on our understanding of its powers and its limitations.

Meade's hope is a judicious hope, one that "can find a way through the gathering darkness." In fact, he suggests that, "Wisdom is not overly hopeful, nor is it subject to overwhelming despair. If it were it wouldn't be very wise."[15]

Hope as a renewable resource: I like it. To begin to see things in this light, or to at least borrow insights from Meade and others, we would need to make some conscious decisions. I'm willing to do that, although research tells me I might not have as much will as I thought I did. How much control do we have in activating such a complex emotional state? On to the neurologists, then. Let's see what the brain scientists have to say.

Notes

1 Hesiod, *Works and Days.*
2 Laertius, *Eminent Philosophers.*
3 Euripides, *Iphigenia.*
4 Shakespeare, *Lucrece.*
5 Franklin, *Poor Richard.*
6 Nietzsche, *Human*, Section 2.
7 Sartre, *Existentialism.*
8 Ibid.
9 Ibid.
10 Ibid.
11 Pope Benedict XVI, *Spe salvi.*
12 Sartre and Lévy, *Hope Now*, 3–42.
13 Raskin, "Camus' Critiques."
14 Meade, "Hidden Hope."
15 Ibid.

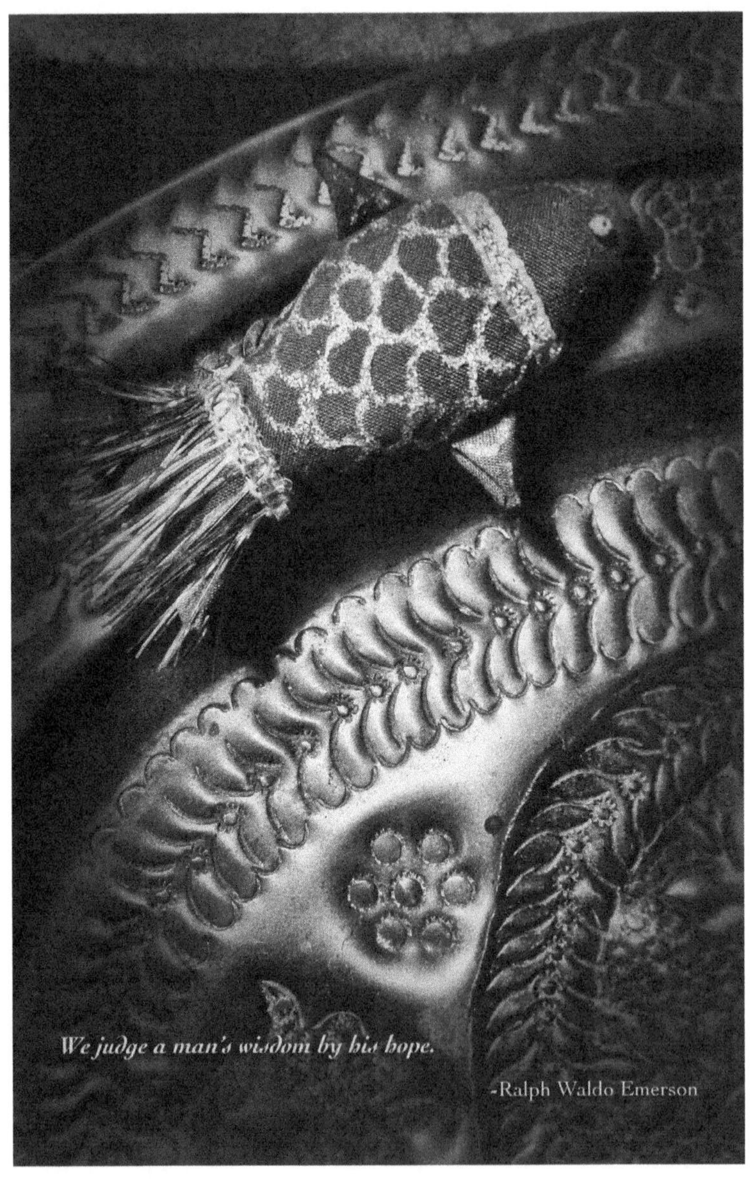
We judge a man's wisdom by his hope.
-Ralph Waldo Emerson

CHAPTER 4

Brain Food

Alvie: I didn't know there was a section of the brain just for hope.
House: It's very, very tiny.
–from Fox TV's *House*

I'm not a neurologist; I barely passed chemistry. Still, I'm fascinated with the brain's potential and its limitations. As I continue to learn more about how we process information, how we act on our impressions, and how we arrive at our most cherished beliefs, I worry. Literature on critical thinking suggests we have a difficult time changing our minds about much of anything. Developing an open mind—reviewing what we think we know, accepting what we don't, and staying as flexible as possible— turns out to be a monumental task. Most of us don't bother cross-checking our confirmation biases, as our tightly held beliefs are called. Science continues to confirm what some of us have long suspected: we are perfectly capable of feeling absolutely certain about ideas and events past, present, and future that aren't supported by fact.

We're making progress in understanding how the brain affects our well-being. Psychological studies about how the brain processes happiness have been around for decades. However, in the last fifteen years or so, neurologists have had the tools to more accurately map brain activity. Using magnetic resonance imaging (MRI) and other devices, scientists can see exactly how our neurotransmitters respond to both physical and emotional stimuli. These images show, for example, that multiple areas of the brain are involved in transmitting the experience of pain. Altering the perception of pain may involve addressing the signals delivered by a particular neurotransmitter. This, in turn, could offer a way to treat not only side effects related to serious illness but also chronic pain itself.

MRI studies have also proven useful in learning where other feelings originate in the brain. A group of Georgetown University researchers discovered that signals are passed from the pre-frontal cortex, where thinking take place, to the nearby pre-motor cortex, which regulates and prepares the body to act. What the images in essence confirm is that both instinct and experience play a part in how we anticipate.[1]

Almost all mammals anticipate on some level; it's a survival mechanism. MRIs have shown the degree to which memory plays a role in human anticipation. Any action we take is preceded by a quick trip through our storehouse of experiences. Animals also make associations that turn them toward or away from activities they determine are either dangerous or gratifying.

Anticipation is sometimes used interchangeably with hope. That's not quite accurate. It may explain, however, why we pet owners assume our animal companions can feel hopeful. Even if they don't look far into the future, we can't help but think there's something going on in the adorable little heads of our favorite furry or feathered buddies. When they stare at us with their soft eyes, aren't they hoping? Aren't they working off some sort of belief system that connects what they desire with a plan to achieve that desire?

Molly, my spaniel-Bichon mix, seems to behave with

calculation. She clearly makes links between sights and sounds, and what might happen next, and what she should do about it. When she hears the garage door open, she reacts with excitement. She connects the sound with either my return or my departure. She always wants to go along. Molly also associates the refrigerator with a treat, since the treats are kept in there. She'll run up to me and then to the refrigerator, then back to me, trying to get me to do something (get the treat out of the refrigerator and into her mouth). Most of the time, I give in to her exuberance, which is pretty hard to resist. But not always. I may open the refrigerator to get food for my lunch. I may open the garage door because I need to run an errand that doesn't include her. When I get ready to leave without her, she appears forlorn; she even turns her head away. I imagine she must be experiencing some sort of emotion, perhaps sadness. What about just prior to that, when she still senses the possibility of an activity that includes her? Is she merely initiating an evolutionary response based on her fixed associations (garage=outside =playtime)? Is something more going on? Is she *hoping* she'll get what she wants? Or is she instinctively reacting to external stimuli?

Measuring animal emotion is as challenging as measuring animal cognition. With the notable exception of certain primates, animals are far more limited in their ability to communicate. In the mid-sixties, a team of psychiatrists ran experiments about "learned helplessness" in dogs, suggesting the findings might serve as a model for studying and treating human depression.[2] The thesis, that learned helplessness was analogous to human depression, was roundly criticized, as was the cruel treatment of the experiment's canine subjects.[3] (A side note: the lead psychologist on the team, Martin

Seligman, was later elected president of the American Psychiatry Association. He also wrote several best-selling motivational books and became a leading proponent of research into the science of happiness.) A 2002 study by scientists with University of Stockholm's zoology department identified five personality traits among dogs.[4] Dr. Jaak Panksepp, author of *Affective Neuroscience: The Foundations of Human and Animal Emotions*, has identified seven core emotions he believes most mammals share, based on measurable reactions.[5] Test results published in 2008 by Dr. Friederike Range, of the University of Vienna's neurobiology department, concluded that dogs can indeed experience more complex emotions such as jealousy, embarrassment, empathy, and guilt.[6]

Although Molly seems more prone to jealousy than empathy, I've seen evidence of both in her. She also anticipates. She gets ready to move just before I throw the ball or runs to the refrigerator when her brain signals hunger. Some of her associations are quite sophisticated (to me), as when she stands in front of the door that opens into the garage whenever I tie up the kitchen trash. She must know I'm getting ready to take it out to the trashcan, which sits in the garage next to the place where her ball is kept. Trash=garage=ball=play-time=wait in front of the door to the garage. Impressive.

Most of Molly's associations, I'd venture to say, are happy ones; she tends to anticipate something rewarding is going to happen. Her tendency to joyful emotions is part of what makes her companionship so gratifying. Anticipation for Molly, however, doesn't always register as positive. Some activities make her excited (We're going to play ball! We're going for a ride! I'm going to get a treat!) Others make her anxious (She's taking me to the vet! She's leaving without me! She's going to yell at me for ripping up the paper!) Happy, sad, joyful, angry or guilty/ distressed: these emotions are available to my pet. I suspect she may even experience something related to affection.

What she doesn't feel is hope.

We often use hope and anticipation interchangeably, but hope goes far beyond action or reaction. Hope involves cognition and a degree of analysis: what should I do that will give me the best chance of achieving the desired outcome? Anticipation involves preparing to act without necessarily thinking about whether the action is logical or optimal. Molly has a particular behavior that actually proves my point. She waits in front of the neighbor's house where, a year earlier, that neighbor gave all the dogs treats. Molly looks longingly at the porch in anticipation of getting a treat (so do the other neighborhood dogs, by the way). She has no context for comprehending that the neighbor is no longer there to hand out treats. She may not even remember why she sits there, only that it has to do with something pleasurable. If she sees someone with a treat, she'll react. But she won't form a plan to achieve her desires, like finding out which neighbors have treats and then walking me past their houses.

I'm actually relieved. I don't need my pet making plans without me.

Identifying the neurological components of hope is far more complicated than working with primary emotions. We'd like to believe that "hope uses the same neurological pathways to heal as does real medication."[7] Cognitive therapy, after all, causes far fewer side effects. But such a declaration may be jumping the gun. For all the excitement about positive thinking and our ability to alter our perceptions, such remedies are not guaranteed to tame pain, let alone illness.

Much has been made of the possibility that positive feelings about how pain is being treated can reduce our pain experience. This is achieved through use of a placebo—a non-drug treatment that might activate the same pain-modulation networks as do conventional drugs. Note I said *might*. The *placebo effect* is "the measurable, observable, or felt improvement in health not attributable to an actual treatment."[8] In research experiments conducted by Columbia University and University of Michigan doctors, patients were found to release more of a natural painkiller in anticipation of relief.[9]

Placebos work in some, but not all, cases. While doctors argue over their value, I'm inclined to think that if one's brain chemistry can be directed to feeling better, why not? We make "subconscious associations between recovery and the experience of being treated,"[10] which can affect the manner in which our immune systems react. If we can trick ourselves into feeling less pain, I'm all for it, as long as we're not subverting pain's primary purpose, which is to warn us when something is wrong.

Neurologists and other science writers (who talk about an *expectation* of relief in patients taking a placebo) are observing quantifiable brain activity instigated by subliminal associations. Researchers now realize that the areas of the brain that release pain-reducing opiates in response to placebos are the same regions that help the brain anticipate the appropriate response in a given situation. What might make a placebo effective is the *anticipation*, not of pain but of relief. The release of helpful chemicals or the reduction of stress can help in coping more effectively with pain.

Does it matter whether we're hoping or anticipating the medicine (or placebo) will work? Do we need to think about automatic responses versus belief systems when all we're doing is seeking relief? Perhaps not, but we do have to recognize what neuroscience can and can't show us about hope on the brain, if for no other reason than to protect ourselves and our loved ones from false claims about the relationship between health and belief. While feelings of hope may be able to persuade the body that something no longer hurts, they aren't likely to address the underlying cause of a serious illness. Hope can help, but only within reason.

Scientists don't really know what a brain on hope looks like. At least one researcher, however, has suggested we can track brain activity for signs of optimism. In *The Optimism Bias,* author Tali Sharot presents the results of several studies conducted by University College London's Wellcome Trust Centre for Neuroimaging, where she is a research fellow. Ms. Sharot, it should be noted, is occasionally confused with Tal Ben Shahar, a psychology professor and motivational lecturer who writes about positive thinking. Shahar's course on happiness was one of the most popular in Harvard University's history. His internationally best-selling books include *Being Happy* and *Happier*.

Sharot excerpted her book for a May 2011 issue of *Time Magazine* on health. I was caught by this paragraph: "After living through Sept. 11, 2001, in New York City, I had set out to investigate people's memories of the terrorist attacks. I was intrigued by the fact that people felt their memories were as accurate as a videotape, while often they were filled with errors. A survey conducted around the country showed that eleven months after the attacks, individuals' recollections of their experience that day were consistent with their initial accounts (given in September 2011) only 63% of the time. They were also poor at remembering details of the event, such as the names of the airline carriers. Where did these mistakes in memory come from?"[11]

Well, several neurologists have written about what our brain fails to remember, which makes the case for self-assessment. Putting aside the question of 9/11 and who would want to remember what, our brains appear to store information less accurately than we'd like to believe. Ah, but Sharot is going further. We do remember, but while our neurons "faithfully encode desirable information that can enhance optimism, [they] fail at incorporating unexpectedly undesirable information." This bias towards optimism is not a flaw, but a way for our memory to produce a vision for the future. It cuts across lines of race, gender, age, culture, and ethnicity. Most of us are optimists, it would seem.

Sharot finds that "both neuroscience and social science suggest that we are more optimistic than realistic."[12] I found it difficult to tell how much neuroscience was part of her equation, although she refers to imaging and brain tracking. At any rate, Sharot describes one experiment, in which the subjects were asked to choose between several pleasant options. They were also told to place an emotional "value" on the choices they made. When asked to narrow their choices, they kept raising the value of those choices. The subjects, we're told, appeared to "derive heightened pleasure from choices that might actually be neutral."[13]

I just thought they were gaming the system.

If they are, it's because they *want* to be uplifted. Perhaps we are inclined to feeling good; it makes perfect evolutionary sense. How do we keep from floating along in a cloud of unreasonable exuberance, though, blind to any information, however helpful, that might spoil our good mood? Sharot addresses these concerns. While an optimism bias is better for our health (happy=healthy), she concedes, "Optimism is also irrational and can lead to unwanted outcomes." What to do? "Knowledge is key," Sharot advises. "We are not born with an innate understanding of our biases. The brain's illusions have to be identified by careful scientific observation and controlled experiments and then communicated to the rest of us. Once we are made aware of our optimistic illusions, we can act to protect ourselves. It is possible, then, to strike a balance, to believe we will stay healthy, but get medical insurance anyway; to be certain the sun will shine, but grab an umbrella on our way out—just in case."[14]

Okay, tempered optimism is what Sharot seems to be offering. Yet even if optimism is instinctive, reasonableness is not. In fact, we tend to believe irrationality is a problem that belongs to the other guy. If, on one hand, we can't loosen our grip on our tightly held assumptions, how can we reign in unfettered optimism? Maybe the question should be: How can we reign in irrational thoughts, whether optimistic or despairing if, at the end of the day, we're slaves to our gut feelings? I appreciate Sharot's optimism about our ability to be happy and logical; I just don't know if we can pull it off.

Given the tendency in all manner of communication to express outrage, amplified by mass media and unconstrained by propriety, reason of any kind might be forgiven for going to ground. For every summons to a shining city on the hill or a promise of change we can believe in, we are presented with hundreds of examples of mudslinging and appeals to mob mentality. Rudeness is recast as honesty; greed is presented as ambition, and lines in the sand blur and move.

For those without the certainty of a happy immortality, instinctive optimism seems impossible to imagine. Not only that, but summoning our inner happy person in the face of various hormones, preconditions, and learned behaviors is not quite a walk in the park.

That's where cognitive therapy is supposed to help. Psychiatry has embraced the idea of hope as an antidote to depression. Since depression is often caught in a dance involving both emotional and physical components, doctors may prescribe both talk therapy and/or medicines to combat despair. Obviously, some severe diseases that manifest themselves as mental illness, like schizophrenia, involve "structural as well as functional brain abnormalities."[15] Talk therapy alone can't help. However, some neurological researchers have concluded talk therapy *can* alter brain function because "learning [new ways to think] leads to the production of new proteins and, in turn, to the remodeling of neurons."[16]

While so much of the brain is beyond our control, we know mental states can be altered. It may not be outrageous to consider hope to be in part a learned behavior. However, it matters who is doing the teaching or coaching, and what they claim their methods can and can't accomplish. Medical professionals are licensed, but not everyone who claims he or she can lift us out of our funk adheres to standards of ethics or, for that matter, common sense. Perhaps the brain can be taught to hope; but it can just as easily be persuaded to fool itself.

Notes

1 Neuroscience, "Wave."

2 Selegman and Maier, "Failure to Escape."

3 Hahner, "Learned Helplessness."
4 Svartberg, et al., "Consistency."
5 Paradiso, "Book Forum."
6 Jamieson, "Dogs."
7 Society for Neuroscience, "Feelings of Hope."
8 Eustice, "Placebo Effect."
9 Physorg.com, "Researchers."
10 Niemi, "Placebo Effect."
11 Sharot, "Optimism Bias."
12 Ibid.
13 Ibid.
14 Ibid.
15 Friedman, "Like Drugs."
16 Ibid.

And so by hoping more, they have but lesse.
-William Shakespeare

CHAPTER 5

HAPPY TALK

False hope really makes you cynical.
–Bill Maher

Tali Sharot proposes a healthy optimism. All we need to do is monitor the brain, indulging its high-wire act while providing a safety net, just in case. Of course, we have to allow for harsh realities, unexpected setbacks, bad days, screwed-up brain chemistry, and other roadblocks on the journey to an upbeat outlook. Maybe it doesn't matter. Optimism seems to be in hiding these days. In the United States in particular, the problem isn't a surfeit of cheer, but the opposite—the dark cloud just above our heads, the black hole that opens beneath our feet. We're in a somber place. Call it apathy, ennui, melancholia, despair, or the blues (I used to call it the "grays"). Whatever it is, it's anything but upbeat.

Traditionally, Americans were hopeful. That hope fueled many of the social advancements in our nation's history. We're apparently not feeling as positive as did our ancestors. Children appear particularly vulnerable to negative thinking. The number of adolescents diagnosed as suffering from depression has been rising. Today five to eight times as many high school and college students meet the criteria for diagnosis of major depression and/or an anxiety disorder as was true half a century or more ago.[1] The cynic in me tends to view these statistics with a large dose of skepticism. After all, diagnosing depression among adolescents has meant more opportunities for pharmaceutical companies to market targeted treatments. That isn't to say depression isn't a problem, only that the relationship between research studies and the concerns that fund them deserves scrutiny [2].

Depression nevertheless needs to be addressed. Talk therapy is one way. Drugs are another. Back in the eighties, when Prozac reigned, the joke was: "Better living through chemistry." While drugs do help with serious psychotic illnesses, they're not a cure-all. The alarming number of prescriptions written (and abused) each year has provoked a reexamination within the mental health profession. Doctors are also coming around to the idea that low serotonin alone isn't necessarily responsible for feelings of depression. Says one Harvard researcher, "Chemical imbalance is sort of last-century thinking."[3]

Enter the positive psychology movement.

Positive psychology has been around awhile. When I was growing up, Norman Vincent Peale was its guru. Peale preached the power of a mindset that credited a high authority, but encouraged individuals to make their own happiness. These days, positive psychology forms a large umbrella under which everyone from medical doctors, psychology professors and licensed therapists to life coaches, motivational speakers and evangelical ministers gather to promote their versions of happiness and mental well-being.

I have nothing against thinking positively. It's a much more pleasant way to live. Most of us don't want to focus only on what's wrong with our lives. We aren't built to be naysayers, at least in Tali Sharot's point of view, and I tend to agree. How to explain this communal negativism, then? I suspect it's caused less by bad news (we've always had bad news) and more by what I call "the expectation clause."

Expectations are as much a part of human psychology as any other complex emotion. They generally arise from the mental calculus we engage in to measure probability and patterns. We regard certain events as likely to happen. We expect the sun to rise in the east because the earth revolves according to a pattern astronomers have been able to track. This pattern remains unchanged over the course of human history. There's no evidence to indicate the earth will stop revolving anytime soon. Something *could* happen, of course; but it would be in the nature of an anomaly. It would be both literally and figuratively earth-shattering. Other natural events—fires that burn, plants that die and bloom cyclically, tides that rise and fall—also conform to our expectations and what we know about earth science.

When we attach expectations to our emotional states, however, we're setting ourselves up for disappointment. If we *expect* a particular outcome and we end up with a different one, if this happens again and again, we also end up with an emotion warehouse filled with frustration.

Everybody expects something; it's human nature. Chronic disappointment, however, is the flip side of relying too heavily on an unrealistic set of expectations. I came across the phrase "chronic disappointment" in an article by a psychiatrist with the delightful name Halcyon Bohen. Dr. Bohen describes the chronically disappointed as "tired, discouraged, stuck, overwhelmed, depleted, ineffective."[4] Bohen also observes resentment and anger in several patients. That sounds like a few people I know. It also seems to describe the societal malaise of the moment. In any event, it's the very opposite of the hope for which the United States was formerly known.

If hope is lost, can it return? If it was never there, can it be instilled? Many cognitive therapists believe so. C.R. Snyder, as I noted earlier, was a proponent of "learned" hope. His methodology is noted for its pragmatic approach to hope as a way of bringing a patient out of severe or chronic depression.

In *The Psychology of Hope: You Can Get There From Here*, Snyder sets out to contradict the common view of hope "as an illusion, totally lacking a basis in reality."[5] He suggests a different kind of hope, a quantifiable mindset that can be developed and nurtured in children and adults alike. It consists of three components: goals (objects, experiences, or outcomes we imagine and desire), willpower ("a reservoir of determination and commitment"), and something called "waypower" (a general belief in our track record of attaining goals combined with the flexibility to seek alternative paths).[6]

To find out how capable an individual is of experiencing a productive version of hope, Snyder introduces a Hope Scale. To see where I might register, I took his simple test. There are eight questions with choices like "definitely false," "mostly false," "mostly true," and "definitely true," with a number between one and four assigned to each, four being the best.

1. I energetically pursue my goals.
2. I can think of many ways to get out of a jam.
3. My past experiences have prepared me well for my future.
4. There are lots of ways around any problem.
5. I've been pretty successful in life.
6. I can think of many ways to get the things in life that are most important to me.

7. I meet the goals that I set for myself.
8. Even when others get discouraged, I know I can find a way to solve the problem.

Because I'm someone who strongly believes in the fourth statement, I answered "definitely true." Other questions caused me some ambivalence, so I "cheated"—I used a 2.5 to land me between mostly false and mostly true. I think that's very enterprising of me, but I'm not sure what that does to my results on the Hope Scale.

I ended up with a score of 24, which is an "average" amount of hope. This seemed to me a positive sign, indicating I had a strong basis for thinking hopefully. Snyder observes that hopeful children make hopeful adults, although non-hopeful children can be taught to hope. Some of us were considered "different" as kids. We didn't fit in. I don't remember being too hopeful as a child, unless I was hoping I'd either grow out of my prickly, fretful self, or find someplace where I'd feel more comfortable. So having an average amount of hope seems promising.

Snyder offers a number of solid and practical (if obvious) suggestions to help us develop a more hopeful outlook: look outward, engage in problem-solving, call on friends, laugh, pray (okay, that one may not work for everyone), exercise, watch our health, and age gracefully (now there's a challenge!). He suggests taking a neutral attitude toward death, which admittedly takes some doing.

Snyder's emphasis on goal-setting is the key to his brand of hope. We naturally set goals for ourselves every day anyway. We need to take ownership of the larger ones and tackle them with "conscious, thoughtful analysis."[7] Sounds like critical thinking, which appeals to me and, probably, would to most die-hard rationalists. Flexibility is another factor in fostering a reasonable sort of hope. This makes absolute sense to me. Flexible hope isn't wimpy; it's practical. Snyder places flexibility and choice into his notion of "waypower." We have choices, he claims, not only in what goals we set for ourselves but also in deciding how to reach them. In Snyder's version of hope, you set a goal and create a process. The process becomes not just a means to an end but a way of living and learning: what is reasonable, what is possible, what the limitations are, of course, but also what the workarounds may be.

I like Snyder's method because it's straightforward and practical. No silly thoughts or magic bullets. No guarantees and no passive waiting around. The primary purpose of learned hope is to overcome depression and provide a means for moving forward. Hope becomes the overarching goal under which one's smaller goals are achieved. In place of an expectation clause, there are sets of guidelines.

Unfortunately, much of the positive psychology movement traffics in expectation. Certain practitioners promulgate the idea that we can harness the untapped portions of our brain to make our wishes come true. We're not talking about setting goals, but about some vague power we can learn to use, something that bends the universe to our will. The specifics of the most extreme positive thinking messages may vary, but the idea is the same. We can get whatever we want by following simple guidelines, which will then unleash our inner winner.

Pandora, meet Narcissus.

I've long been squeamish about the idea that we can dictate outcome via willpower. I don't know everything about the brain, except that we don't use all of it. Then again, neither do those who promote this version of positive thinking. That hasn't stopped the "getting what you want in three easy steps" people from cashing in on the dreams and, yes, entitlement fantasies of those who feel they're not getting what they deserve. Take *The Secret*. Borrowing freely from sources as varied as Norman Vincent Peale, the Old Testament, and *The Celestine Prophecy*, the book purports to let us in on a little secret. The rich and powerful are rich and powerful because they know how to get what they want. This foolproof prescription for living tells us, shows us in fact that what attracts us most—wealth, fame, power, security—is what will be attracted to us. We want money, we focus on money; we have money. Simple as that.

The focus on material gain is in line with the times, or perhaps with all times. Wealth brings power and influence, control, and the ability to buy visibility or isolation, respect, or freedom. The book also exhibits a particular kind of callousness when it comes to failure. If things *aren't* working out in your favor, if you suffer from financial reversals or are deathly ill, for example, you're not trying hard enough. Even that suggestion mirrors the prevailing ruthlessness of the marketplace.

The effect of the book's message on "regular" people varies. Some people claim to use what they need, and ignore the sillier details. But others have taken the mind over matter theme far too literally. In 2007, one of Oprah Winfrey's admirers decided Winfrey's enthusiastic endorsement of the book meant the advice would work in all instances. The woman reportedly decided to forgo post-cancer treatment in favor of directing positive energy out to the universe. While thinking good thoughts is undoubtedly easier than going through chemotherapy, the decision was medically questionable, to say the least. Fortunately, the cancer patient wrote Winfrey a letter, and the talk show host devoted a show to reasoning with the book's more ardent followers, urging them to remember that positive energy alone might not solve every problem.

The book's acolytes continue to preach the gospel of *The Secret*. My sister was out to dinner not long ago with friends, including her close buddy, Sue. Sue was bravely dealing with a virulent form of cancer that would eventually kill her. One of the guests that night suggested that maybe Sue's attitude had caused her cancer: negative energy= negative outcome. Talk about bad karma! I heard later that the only sound in the room was the scraping of my sister's chair as she rose. I think she intended to punch the guest in the face but was restrained.

We can laugh or gasp or shake our heads at the thoughtlessness of such remarks. Consider this, however: Proselytizing comes far more naturally to many of us than critical thinking. Once we think something makes sense, there's no shaking us loose from our convictions. Positive psychology in particular has such a benevolent aspect. What could possibly be wrong with encouraging people to look on the bright side?

Not everyone is upbeat and some writers suggest not everyone has to be. Julie K. Norem is a staunch defender of what she calls "defensive pessimism" as both a business strategy and a coping mechanism. "Defensive pessimism involves learning to tolerate negative emotions in order to get things done,"[8] she instructs us. Thinking pessimistically and planning for the worst, she adds, is a valid way to control anxiety. In fact, learning to tolerate bad feelings provides a crucial life lesson. We gain insight from our mistakes. Furthermore, we're better able to listen to constructive criticism, and effectively assess risk. Norem points to business successes who were pessimists, and assures us that we don't all have to believe everything will work out for the best. As for coping with negative feelings, defensive pessimism is actually a way to avoid depression.

The phrase "defensive pessimism" makes me laugh. I thought that being realistic about life's perils and pitfalls was good enough. Apparently, though, "defensive pessimism" can benefit those who are likely to worry anyway. If you're going to get anxious about your upcoming meeting, turn it into an advantage and have a backup plan for your web-based presentation.

By far the most stinging rebuttal of the notion of the positive thinking movement comes via Barbara Ehrenreich, whose *Bright-Sided: How Positive Thinking Is Undermining America* is something of a wake-up call. Ehrenreich points out the movement's negative effect on not only the medical profession, but all aspects of American culture. Positive thinking, she asserts, is promoted as the answer to a public worried about the future and fearful of uncertainty. The idea of being able to will things to be better is what drives the motivational industry. Yet that outlook is the very essence of self-deception because it adheres to the idea that "things are getting better" in the face of evidence things clearly are not.[9]

Ehrenreich sees "consumer capitalism" as having capitulated to positive psychology. We've literally bought into the idea that there will always be enough to buy and enough money to buy it. She makes a convincing case in her chapter, "How Positive Thinking Destroyed the Economy," that supercharged confidence kept many insiders, who should have known better, from paying attention to warning signs. Her book came out well in advance of the latest post-Occupy Wall Street essays on the market's irrational exuberance, which suggests she was prescient in identifying a deeper strain of unconstrained optimism.

In her chapter, "God Wants You to Be Rich," Ehrenreich worries about the confluence of faith and get-rich expectations. The mega-churches operate like corporations, she asserts, with marketing plans, public relations experts, number-crunching, and targeted membership goals. The churches' own market research has shown that members don't want to be harangued about sin. Positive thinking is a natural fit. Faith, at least in the United States, is intertwined with an economic motif that Ehrenreich describes as a "God wants you to succeed" theology.[10] As televangelist Joyce Meyer is quoted as saying, "I believe God wants to give us nice things."[11]

The motivational industry's influence within the medical and science communities is what Ehrenreich views as especially loathsome. She refers to the cancer cure "industry" and lambasts the pink ribbon campaign as falsely cheerful. Ehrenreich, a breast cancer survivor, resents the insistence on being upbeat as demeaning. "The sugar-coating of cancer can exact a dreadful cost [because] first, it requires the denial of understandable feelings of anger and fear."[12] While she acknowledges, "a 'positive attitude' is supposedly essential to recovery,"[13] she notes that "There is no consistent evidence that willpower alone can cure cancer, and considerable evidence drawing the opposite conclusion."[14]

Ehrenreich isn't alone in cautioning about the limits of positivism as a cure-all. Many years ago, I happened upon an article in a men's magazine about the relationship between health and attitude. I was struck by a caveat that appeared up front in the editor's note: Sometimes biology trumps psychology. Those who urge caution are dismissed as cynics and naysayers. More often than not, however, the enthusiastic proponents of the all-powerful mind need to be reminded that optimism can't do it all. A positive outlook won't cure disease or prevent death.

More recently, Abraham Verghese, the author of *Cutting for Stone* and a professor at Stanford University Medical Center, lambasted "a cottage industry of books and a cult of author- gurus [that] feed the idea that the correct amount of faith or laughter or visualization or quantum thinking or 'natural' drugs are critical to beating cancer."[15] Not only is such a view scientifically unsupported, he points out, but he also confirms what Ehrenreich discovered. Patients "feel they must be optimistic...and deny those moments when they are dispirited or pessimistic."[16]

Ehrenreich references *The Secret* and its central theme, that what we put to the universe as our desires will come back to us. She is rightly furious that the positive thinking culture embraces this idea as "science." In presentations like one she attended called, "Our Unlimited Minds," the speakers use "fake quantum physics" to demonstrate how we can create brain waves to affect outcomes. Ehrenreich attempts to challenge the bogus science, only to be told by one "life coach" that perhaps the "method" simply doesn't work for Ehrenreich.

Ehrenreich reserves her most withering scorn for the psychiatric profession. She deplores the efforts of the American Psychiatric Association, beginning in 1997, to legitimize studies of happiness under its then leader Martin Seligman.[17] Since these studies tapped into "a rich, nurturing steam of foundation money," it may have been a smart business move on the part of the APA, she says. She questions the scholarly value of academic studies on happiness. They exist, she suspects, so that positive psychology proponents can lay claim to authenticity via the overused phrase, "studies show."

The Templeton Foundation is one of Ehrenreich's targets. Templeton is a big supporter of "positive psychology" research. Ehrenreich criticizes its espousal of free enterprise as a definitive solution to the ills of the world. Templeton is strongly supported by religious and political conservatives. Several philosophers and scientists such as Richard Dawkins have also found Templeton's recent attempts to add a scientific patina to its work to be deceitful. Dawkins shared correspondence between Professor Anthony Grayling and a science journalist who invited him to participate in a conference held by Templeton. Grayling wrote, "I cannot agree with the Templeton Foundation's project of trying to make religion respectable by conflating it with science; this is like mixing astrology with astronomy or voodoo with medical research, and I disapprove of Templeton's use of its great wealth to bribe compliance with this project."[18]

Like Norem, Ehrenreich likes the idea of defensive pessimism. She doesn't equate it with despair either, but rather with the sort of pragmatic caution that makes the pursuit of happiness possible. I agree with Ehrenreich in theory, although her "vigilant realism" feels a bit punishing, like a cold shower after a night of hard partying.

Anyway, we've all presumably been injected with a large dose of reality since Ehrenreich's book came out in 2008. We've been smacked down and pulled back from our more excessive enthusiasms. We've been scolded about our irrational faith in our economy. We're much more cynical than we were even at the beginning of the twenty-first century. Satire is making a strong showing, with plenty of material on which to riff. "Cancer comedy"—an entertainment subgenre that gained traction after Julie Sweeney's one-woman show, *God Said "Ha!,"*[19] and has been represented by both the 2011 movie *50/50* and the Showtime series *The Big C*—rejects both despair *and* upbeat cheerfulness in favor of an attitude that combines anger, disbelief, and the weirdly empowering opportunity to be as outrageous as you please. We're not upbeat; we're snarky.

Positive thinking is still big business. A cursory trip around the Web reveals that the motivational industry is alive and very well. The Happiness Institute offers franchise opportunities for business coaching. *The Secret* continues to sell well around the world. The happiness studies scorned by Ehrenreich continue to receive funding. The American Psychiatric Association profiled a University of California psychologist with a five-year, one million-dollar grant to conduct research on what makes people happy. Dr. Sonja Lyubomirsky and her colleagues are using the National Institute of Health grant to "[explore] the potential of happiness-sustaining strategies."[20] One of the researchers' preliminary conclusions is that forty percent of our happiness may be within our control if we can learn to limit our "over-thinking."

Who knew over-thinking could be quantified?

Though I enjoyed the Ehrenreich book, she makes what I consider to be a giant misstatement at the beginning of the book when she defines optimism as "a cognitive stance, a conscious expectation, which presumably anyone can develop through practice," and hope as nothing more than an emotional response, a yearning "not entirely within our control."[21] Ehrenreich gets it exactly backward, optimism being a primary emotion, and hope being a more complex state of mind that is at least, in part, cognitive. Still, I appreciate her tart warnings about the dangers of the motivational industry. The positive psychology movement has its fair share of charlatans.

The interview with Lyubomirsky, on the other hand, left me feeling not happy but irritable. That was even before I noted she was a winner of the 2002 Templeton Positive Psychology Prize. I'm sure many of us could stand to adjust our thinking to allow for greater happiness. When Lyubomirsky indicates the path to happiness might be reached if we "limit our over-thinking,"[22] I realize she might be urging us to ease up on self-analysis or curtail our long internal monologues about what we're supposed to be accomplishing with our lives. Maybe she's simply recommending we tamp down our more obsessive thoughts. Sometimes some of us worry too much, or forget to prioritize, or take the weight of the world's problems on our shoulders.

On the other hand, I'm sensitive to any suggestion that thinking and feeling interfere with one another. That tired trope underscores some of the elements of New Age spiritualism as well; and it bothers me. Deep thinking does not necessarily result in unhappiness. I know some people (raises hand) whose hackles might rise if told, "Your problem is you think too much."

Positive psychology in a strictly therapeutic form has many benefits for chronically depressed people. It provides a guide for exiting the darkness of despair with methods and exercises that help the patient refocus. In Snyder's version of hope, the idea of control comes into play. The patient sets goals and builds a process by which to achieve them. This is not simply idle make-work. The effort of creating one's own process becomes not just a means to an end, but something more: a way of learning how to exert some control, develop some flexibility, and understand what is reasonable and what is possible.

Unfortunately, too many of the "happy talkers" appear to be ill equipped to tackle either the neurological or emotional components of a reasonably positive outlook. Their advice ranges from simplistic to scientifically and psychologically untenable...and it's the most vulnerable people who pay the price. Any workable form of hope has to divest itself from the twin anchors of expectation and certainty in order to stay strong and flexible in the face of life's obstacles.

Notes

1 Gray, "Dramatic Rise."
2 Edwards, "Big Pharma's."
3 Spiegel, "Serotonin."
4 Bohen, "Treating."
5 Snyder, *Psychology of Hope*, 2.
6 Ibid., 6–9.
7 Ibid., 215.
8 Norem, *Positive Power*, 95.
9 Ehrenreich, *Bright-Sided*, 5.
10 Ibid., 137.
11 Ibid., 140.
12 Ibid., 41.
13 Ibid., 33.
14 Ibid., 39.
15 Verghese, "Hope and Clarity."
16 Ibid.
17 Ehrenreich, *Bright-Sided*, 147, 148.
18 Richard Dawkins Foundation, "Correspondence."

19 Sweeney, *God Said "Ha!"*
20 Lyubomirsky, "Happiness Diet."
21 Ehrenreich, *Bright-Sided*, 4.
22 Lyubomirsky, "Happiness Diet."

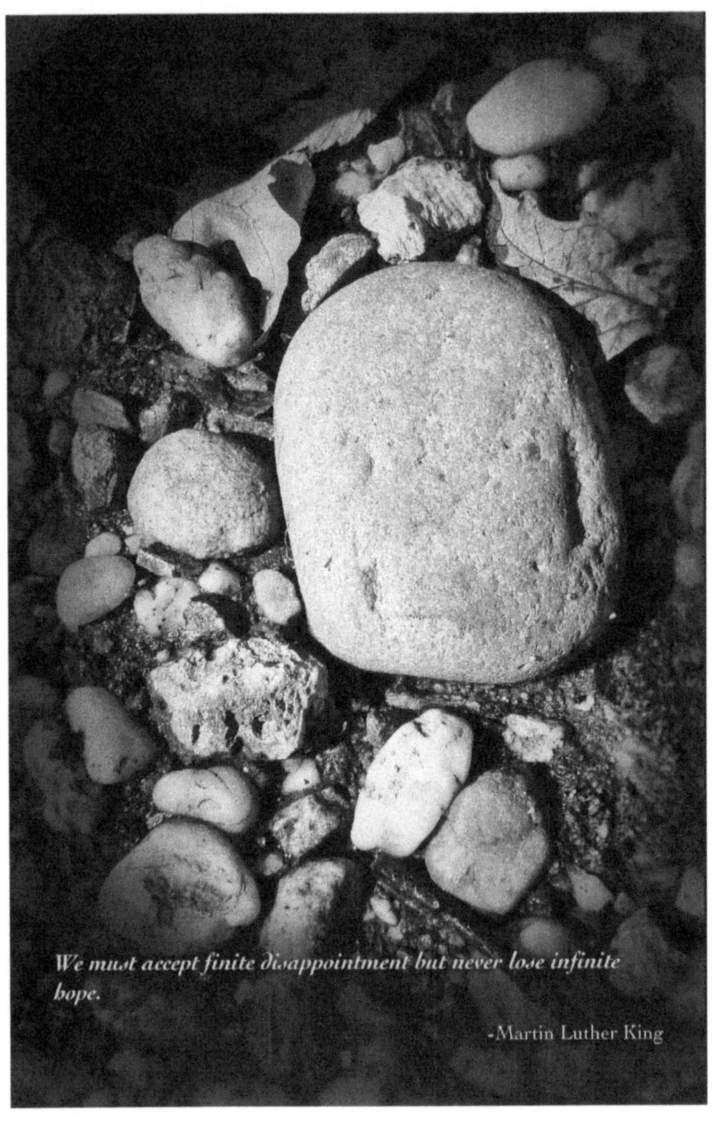
We must accept finite disappointment but never lose infinite hope.
-Martin Luther King

CHAPTER 6

STUFF HAPPENS

The pessimist sees difficulty in every opportunity. The optimist sees the opportunity in every difficulty.
–Winston Churchill

One of the most famous slogans of the late sixties and early seventies was given a marvelous fictional back-story in the movie *Forrest Gump*. The lead character is something of an idiot savant with the uncanny ability to be in the center of history. In one scene, a young man trying to make his own mark looks to Forrest Gump for inspiration:

> Bumper Sticker Guy: [running after Forrest] "Hey, man! Hey, listen, I was wondering if you might help me. 'Cause I'm in the bumper sticker business and I've been trying to think of a good slogan, and since you've been such a big inspiration to the people around here, I thought you might be able to help me jump into—WHOA! Man, you just ran through a big pile of dog shit!"
> Forrest Gump: "It happens."
> Bumper Sticker guy: "What? Shit?"
> Forrest Gump: "Sometimes."[1]

This memorable scene gives us a fanciful version of the origins and subsequent popularity of the phrase "Sh*t happens." The problem is that it doesn't tell us *why* it happens.

Of all the inane, insane, well-intentioned, but ultimately meaningless things people said to me after my husband died in the World Trade Center attacks, that phrase made the most sense to me. It was delivered by a plain-spoken neighbor whose friend may or may not have administered a swift kick under the table after she said it. But it rang true. Horrible, unexpected, inexplicable, unfair, cruel things happen to people, good people; ordinary people going about their business and trying to live decent lives.

It's tempting to look to the sky and demand an explanation from whatever one believes is up there pulling strings. Some people find the idea of a grand master plan comforting, until that plan becomes incomprehensible. All of us directly affected by 9/11 were taken aback at having been caught up in an unforeseeable event. Terrorism, we thought, happened to other people in other parts of the world. Naïve, perhaps, but the shock compounded our grief.

Imagine the further blow dealt to those who also felt betrayed by a god who allowed such an awful thing to happen. "How could God do this to us?" cried a relative on 9/11. His anguish was heartfelt and horrific, made more so by his expectation that his god would never so grievously hurt a faithful follower. I would have preferred to be spared from pain, but I never assumed anyone was responsible for either sparing or causing me that pain, except those who planned and carried out the attacks. My refusal to blame God, blame the universe, or blame anyone didn't make my emotional injury less severe, but it might have protected me from the tumult of an upended belief system.

Everyone experiences disappointments, and sometimes far worse odds that make a simple disappointment look like a blessing. Sometimes bad seems to rule the day.

Now and then the advantage will go to the other guy, who might deserve his good fortune, but might also be a greedy so-and-so or a good-for-nothing louse.

Unfair? As my dad used to say, "Fair is a description of the weather."

Good things happen, too: love, birth, success, or an unexpected opportunity. We get what we think we deserve—what we planned for, worked for, or sacrificed for. Perhaps we decide that ducking misfortune is its own kind of luck. I've been known to offer thanks for missing a horrible or even an onerous obligation. On the other hand, I don't believe my fortune means I was granted a dispensation that day, just as I don't believe some of us are "supposed" to suffer. I can't conceive of a supernatural force that decides on a daily basis who gets the short end of the stick, or even one that strikes capriciously whenever the urge hits it. To me, such an image is far more disturbing than accepting a random world.

Sh*t happens. Life is random. Great; what are we supposed to do with that information?

Plenty of people think they know how to advise us. On *Beliefnet.com*, author and psychologist Terese Borchard lists twenty-one ways we can overcome disappointment. Some of these are both creative and practical, such as, "Throw away the evidence," or "Ignore the critics."[2] Others, like "Dance in the rain," seem to belong to the "When life hands you lemons, make lemonade," school of thought. I find those sorts of recommendations less than useful. It's not that I require specificity when it comes to guidance, but I'm not always in a "turn your frown upside down" frame of mind.

News programs often choose "feel good" stories that feature physically disabled or seriously ill people coping brilliantly. I'm always stunned to see images of immobilized people creating art or becoming activists for their disabilities, as the actor Christopher Reeve did following a paralyzing riding accident. How the hell does that person get out of bed? What motivates him or her to keep going? Like most of us, I assume—no, I believe—I'd never be able to duplicate those efforts.

No one knows what allows some people to overcome disability or situational adversity. We may not even comprehend when we talk about "overcoming" a setback. Nor are we privy to the private doubts and moments of despair with which even the most resolute person grapples. Besides, one individual, while awe-inspiring, can't be a template for anyone and everyone in similar situations. We all suffer differently, just as we all grieve differently.

When Ehrenreich wrote about her personal experiences as a breast cancer survivor, she focused on the way cancer's culture of cheerfulness promotes "the denial of understandable feelings of anger and fear."[3] Encouraging women not to feel like victims is important. It's also crucial to remember there is no one way to deal with or handle illness, loss, or any other bad news.

Society tends to forget that. Even the term "setback" is invariably joined with the word "temporary," as if everything were simply a hold-up, a blip along life's pathway. We expect the grieving, ill, or otherwise challenged person is going to kick the thing to the curb. The only question is when.

Just as there is no one approach to the sh*t life throws at us, neither is there a timeline beyond which we're suddenly all better. One dramatic event can impact the rest of our lives. Obviously, we have to deal with the shock or grief or disappointment to the best of our abilities. *How* we go about doing this, or how long it takes, may vary. To this day, I'm amazed by the number of people who expressed concern at my level of pain after my husband died, or astonishment at my expressions of hope. What they didn't understand or couldn't see was that everything was up in the air—pain, healing, despair, hope, possibility, fury, and some attempts to be funny. I was trying to untangle my own needs; I couldn't deal with societal expectations. If I was moving forward, it felt as if I were moving through molasses. My process incorporated plenty of rage, lots of profanity, copious amounts of tears, buckets of black humor, and any number of emotional missteps. Socially acceptable? Who gives a sh*t?

Setbacks are painful. Sometimes they're avoidable, as when we stubbornly pursue a goal we should have realized was a bad idea. Nonhuman animals can't always learn from experience, which is why certain species have been known to throw themselves repeatedly at immovable barricades until they kill themselves. They don't have the capacity to assess the situation, see what isn't working, and make adjustments. Animals with higher levels of cognitive abilities can learn from their experiences. Sometimes they need help to remember; but, generally, they're unlikely to return to behavior that harms them. Well, except us, silly humans.

Fools rush in where angels fear to tread, and we do, too, chasing impossible goals, falling in love with unavailable partners, repeating behavior we should have learned won't get us what we want. I was once asked if I thought I would have been better off not falling in love with my husband, as if I could have helped it. Please. Sh*t happens.

There are people who feel emotional isolation is the way to go. It seems impossible to me, but I have friends who believe they can control how much pain or disappointment they have in their lives. I don't happen to think that's any way to live life, but it's not mine to live, it's theirs. Others simply try to minimize the worst imaginable by taking precautions. Parents control where their children play or who they play with. Pet owners keep Kitty inside and keep Fido on a leash. I have friends who avoid online transactions or avoid using email. I'm all for common sense if it brings comfort and doesn't inconvenience anyone.

Most of us assume that, if we just keep our heads down, we're safe. Not true. I once told my husband that I felt sometimes as if we lived "beneath the radar" because we tended not to draw attention to ourselves in public. Now I know there's no such thing. No one, whether a public figure or a hard-working guy with a family to support, is truly safe from the event for which we can't plan. A little-known virus, a random accident, or a terrorist attack will change lives in an instant. Sometimes the best-laid plans simply don't produce the desired outcome.

Ready to toss hope in the trashcan? Not so fast.

Reasonable hope encourages us to set goals that allow us to feel connected and purposeful. The goals have to be flexible, however. There's nothing like a series of life-changing disappointments to force you into a decision: try living without hope or adopt a flexible version. I can't manage the first. I'd venture to say most people can't, and I don't think anyone should. But we're trying to be practical here, and reason dictates we focus on moving forward and adapting to setbacks. Sometimes challenges present opportunities. Other times, they provide valuable lessons.

I once planned to be a professional musician, songwriter who might one day head to the mailbox outside her country home to collect royalty checks. My career was launched in Washington, DC, because that's where I finished graduate studies in something altogether different. The music community was small and close-knit. I played cocktail hour at area hotels, one of the ubiquitous lounge singers patrons tend to ignore while having drinks with colleagues after work. I worked occasional gigs with my then boyfriend. I did a bit of jingle-writing and recording; I composed for a children's theater group. Many of my fellow musicians were alumni of the Army, Navy, and Marine bands. They worked all the time. During the day, they taught. At night, they played. When they had free time, they jammed together. They managed to balance work with life. Their families all hung out on the weekends, playing baseball or football, barbecuing, challenging each other to games of Trivial Pursuit. While music news in the seventies was dominated by the drug-fueled exploits of the touring superstars, I was happily ensconced in my music cocoon, writing and working and stretching the heck out of each dollar. I was dead broke and deliriously happy.

Then my boyfriend decided to move to New York, and I followed. It seemed logical, since there really wasn't enough work in Washington. Maybe New York is simply something every creative person has to try. At any rate, we moved, and he went to work immediately as a reliable hire for the Broadway show circuit. Occasionally, he went on tour. Meanwhile, although I worked hard for the next ten years, I couldn't get a toehold. The coveted session gigs were fiercely guarded, the musical theater workshops filled with determined young writers. The entire music scene was changing. Ambitious composers set up home studios and worked in solitude on their various projects. My musician and partner left, taking with him his musical friends as well as the sense of camaraderie. For a while I worked on theatrical shows, restoring my sense of community within the context of specific projects. I wasn't having fun. I was still dead broke, but far less deliriously happy. Even the afterschool program I worked with as "composer in residence" was less joyful, more fraught, in a rough neighborhood, and constantly threatened by budget cuts. I had some wonderful experiences in the eighties in New York, but I spent far too much time alone and afraid. By the time I met my soon-to-be husband, I had concluded that I had no future as a professional musician.

It's funny to realize how strongly I'd hoped for a career in music, and how much it cut me to be "rejected' by a fickle business. Maybe I could have played the clubs for a while, or gone back for a teaching degree, but that's not what I was after. I wanted to compose and get paid a living wage for it. I also wanted to stay connected to other musicians. After fifteen years, I had to accept that wasn't going to happen. I struggled along for a couple of years, then turned my back on music altogether for a time. In retrospect, it was a silly step to take, like refusing to talk with someone who didn't even know he'd hurt your feelings—and my feelings were hurt. I'd invested so much time and energy, and so much passion in music, I couldn't imagine a life that didn't center on making it a career. All my eggs had been in that basket.

Then I met the man I'd marry. Transferring a whole host of hopes, dreams, emotional needs and desires seemed the natural thing to do. I took a "real" job, settled into married life, coped with bouts of restlessness, and lived happily ever after. Except I didn't.

Twelve years later, he was dead, killed in a terrorist attack I could not possibly have foreseen.

Full stop.

Sh*t happens. Good sh*t and bad sh*t. There's no rhyme or reason, no master plan. I know some people believe things happen for a reason. I don't see it that way. Things just happen. As the Borg in the long-lived *Star Trek* series like to say, "Resistance is futile."[4] If you can't plan for the unforeseeable, how do you plan at all? How can you possibly look *forward* to anything?

The most valuable skill I developed as a musician wasn't my ability to read music or sing in any style. What I learned to do when studying and playing jazz was to improvise. If music is about form and structure, left-brain stuff, then improvisation is the ultimate in intuitive creative flow. At the same time, you never stop thinking, but your focus is less on the details than on the big picture. When you improvise, you give yourself (your brain) permission to do whatever is necessary to create something within the structures of something else. It's really a type of puzzle-solving: How do I get from here to there (and back again)? True improvisation requires you to know the rules, to understand both the opportunities and limits of the structure. In musical terms, you introduce the melody before you play around with it. In jazz parlance, as my vocal coach Howard Roberts always reminded me, you "play the head; then riff."

The thing that made improvisation so enjoyable for me was the unpredictability of the inner journey, the tune within the tune. Improvisation isn't life-threatening, not even potentially devastating, but it carries its own musical risks. The best musicians like to walk out on the ledge, to the point where the listener has to trust the player to find his or her way back... because one way or another, you always come back.

I liked the on-the-fly creativity, the trick of working in new melodies that paid homage to the original, all the while playing and moving the song along. I'm not sure musicians think they're so much "improving" on a tune when they improvise as embellishing, expanding, and using that tune as a springboard for their own journeys. The improvised portion, the "song within the song," is an added bonus for the listeners that pushes the outer boundaries while also paying tribute to and respecting the "what is," the main melody.

Life requires improvisation more than we'd like to imagine. We know we're born, we live, and we die. We make plans and do our best to follow through, and that makes things mostly easier; but sometimes we're detoured anyway. Some things appear predetermined, and some events are more likely to happen to people in one demographic or statistical subset than in another. Some people begin with more advantages; others acquire (or lose) advantage as they go along. Environment and heredity work as predictors with great success. It helps to figure out as much as we can and to establish for ourselves a comfortable core set of beliefs that can grow, and expectations that can adapt.

Adaptation is crucial, whether it involves plans or assumptions. Hope tied to certainty will trip us up every time. There's no reason to expect fair treatment or the best possible outcome. On the other hand, there's every reason to work for it. Reasonable hope requires flexibility, because life requires flexibility. Sh*t happens. Hope hides. Then it adapts—or dies.

As I write this, I've learned a dear friend has a neurological disease. After spending several years in denial rather than in treatment, his version has gotten pretty advanced. To say that's a setback is to put it mildly. It's a boulder in the road; a fruit basket upset. How does he cope? What can he expect? What can he do? He's in unfamiliar territory. In musical terms, he's off the sheet, away from the head, and more or less on his own. Now what?

In typical fashion, my friend has read dozens of books and papers, and sought out advice and guidance from professionals and friends alike. He's had some pretty awful days while the doctors try out different drugs and therapies. He's riding a roller coaster of emotions, of course. He's also making discoveries about himself that I find nothing short of miraculous. He's decided to *own* his disease, chronicle it, write about every aspect of it for as long as he can and, at the same time, let his life take him where it will take him. He's become creative and has upped his output impressively. He's planning ahead, yes, but he's also staying loose.

"I'm making it up as I go along, Nikki," he tells me. Well, aren't we all?

In any improvisation session, certain elements are pre-determined. The framework will begin with some givens, as well as a purpose and a goal. Certain outcomes are known, just as in life. Within the constraints, however, there are lots of possibilities, obstacles, or detours that make up a process that's both informed and unpredictable. We end up with the freedom to make up our own music as we go along.

Notes

1 Paramount, *Forrest Gump*.

2 Borchard, "Twenty-One Ways."

3 Ehrenreich, *Bright-Sided*, 41.

4 The Borg from Star Trek: Next Generation (1986–1994) to express their ability to dominate opponents. Star Trek Database.

Hope is the physician of each misery.
-Old Irish proverb

CHAPTER 7

Make It Stop Hurting

Pain is inevitable. Suffering is optional.
–Author Unknown

Lower back, both hips (even though they've both been replaced), right ankle and left shoulder. Most every day, some part of my body is giving me a hard time. My discomfort is constant, although it varies from annoying to much worse. Weather affects the pain. Activity or lack of activity both factor in. Sometimes my enthusiasm gets the better of me, and I run my dog. Sometimes I'm hard at work writing and forget to stand up. In either instance, I pay with pain.

I'm not alone. Paying with pain is a common occurrence, resulting in everything from mood changes to lost productivity. Chronic pain in particular is a drain on individuals, their families and the economy as a whole.

Laura suffers from migraines that can sideline her for hours, sometimes days at a time. Amy puts up with psoriasis and painful joint swelling. Both migraine headaches and psoriasis are autoimmune diseases, as are rheumatoid arthritis and fibromyalgia. The pain can be excruciating; it's often nonspecific, impossible to relieve by simply getting off your feet or icing your hands.

While autoimmune disorders affect people in every age group, including children, they fall most heavily on women. Three times as many women as men suffer from debilitating migraine headaches.[1] In fact, of the 110 million or so Americans who are suffering from all types of chronic pain,[2] the majority are women.[3] For years, the gender discrepancy was attributed solely to hormones, along with societal assumptions about men, women, and emotions. Women felt chronic pain more often than men, we were told, because women supposedly lacked the rigor to overcome their "mental/emotional" issues. Pain was lumped together with other "nervous" disorders likely to be suffered by women. (Take to your beds, ladies, and pass the laudanum.)

More recently, researchers have noted biological differences between women and men that affect pain perception. One study found the presence of a greater density of nerve receptors in the female body.[4] Research has also shown that some women, including those with fibromyalgia, may be lacking an adaptive mechanism that limits the amount of pain the brain can handle.[5]

According to a 2011 *Time Magazine* series on health, more than 76,000,000 Americans feel pain that lasts days, weeks—or longer.[6] On the whole, the brain works as the body's beat cop, monitoring its well-being and warning us to take protective action when necessary, i.e., pull the hand out of the flame, run away, stop running, sit up, or sit down. But when pain is a response unrelated to any obvious illness or malfunction, it becomes its own disorder. The Institute of Medicine of the National Academies has recognized chronic pain as distinct from an active or ongoing disorder or disease.[7] In a sign chronic pain is being taken seriously, the Institute has also called for "coordinated, national efforts of public and private organizations to create a cultural transformation in how the nation understands and approaches pain management and prevention," and a recommendation that the National Institutes of Health "designate a lead institute to move pain research forward and increase the scope and resources of its existing Pain Consortium."[8]

New research makes it clear just how devastating chronic pain is to the brain. Researchers can now confirm that a brain experiencing chronic pain looks different on an MRI from a "normal" brain.[9] The differences can become permanent, which perpetuates the vicious cycle. Other discoveries are also revealing; for instance, that chronic pain sufferers have lower than normal endorphin levels in their spinal fluid (endorphins are natural pain suppressants).[10]

Doctors are heard to say they're "hopeful" about new treatments for chronic pain. I'm reserving judgment. For one thing, chronic pain (CP in medical jargon) isn't curable, only manageable. Sufferers are faced with options that entail using drugs, including those that suppress the immune system, and/or attempting the euphemistic "lifestyle modification." That in turn can mean anything from getting more rest to completely restructuring your life around your incapacitation, which is not an option for most working Americans. Those who live with chronic pain will attest to its power to disable them. It attacks not only the body but the mind, leaving the sufferer weak, vulnerable, and unable to fully concentrate. CP is also one of the costliest health problems in the United States, with an estimated annual price tag of close to fifty billion dollars.[11]

Pain is real. The fact that it's in our brain doesn't make it a wholly psychological process, or a wholly physical one. Rather, pain involves a tangled mix of cause and effect, with sensations setting off physical changes in the brain, which then produces more unpleasant sensations. Treating it, a doctor friend of mine once suggested, is like chasing an enemy through a maze, an enemy who is always one or two steps ahead. When not traced to an obvious physical ailment, pain might show up anywhere. As for how pain is registered by different brains, imagine two gunshot victims or two arthritis patients who simply don't hurt the same. Beyond the physical symptoms, how are they to be treated?

It helps to understand how pain works. Physicians describe it as falling into three categories. **Somatic pain** is the most common, occurring in the musculoskeletal system—the skin, bones, muscles, ligaments, tendons, and joints. **Neuropathic pain** comes from nerve damage (carpal tunnel syndrome is an example). **Visceral pain** is generally short-lived, like the pain women experience during menstruation or labor. Sometimes pain defies categorization, as when everything seems to hurt. Sometimes two kinds of pain appear at the same time.[12] No wonder diagnosis and treatment are so challenging.

Most people hate to be in pain. We're at the mercy of something we can't control. At least I recognize pain as something that can be managed. I get annoyed by pain charts with emoticons on a one-to-ten scale. Do I feel more like a smiley two (lower pain) or am I edging towards ten, a full-on frown? On the other hand, I realize the chart acts as the doctor's assistant. It helps to pinpoint essential questions like how much does the pain interfere with your ability to take care of yourself? If the faces help the doctor, they help me.

What the chart can't do is separate the psychological from the physical. Most chronic pain sufferers bristle at the suggestion that their pain might be related to their attitude, and no wonder. We women in particular are sensitive to hints that we're behaving like drama queens about pain. Still, doctors need to take into consideration everything from a patient's genetic makeup to her past experiences. Moreover, pain is linked to depression in both directions. Childhood depression may cause adults to experience the physical symptoms of pain.[13] Constant pain can change the brain as well, creating a loop of negative emotions feeding negative sensations, which further focus us on our pain. The affected areas of the brain "are stuck on full throttle, wearing out neurons and altering their connections to each other." The faulty equilibrium "can change the wiring forever and could hurt the brain."[14]

This not likely to produce hopeful feelings, unless there's something we can do about it.

Today's medical professionals advocate a balanced approach to pain management that combines pharmaceutical and non-drug therapies. These don't have to be dire choices if incorporated thoughtfully. Drug-induced pain relief has taken a public relations hit in recent years. Some of it is deserved; some is not. The more addictive opiates like Oxycontin, along with certain anti-anxiety medicines, have spawned a gray market, with patients and doctors abusing prescriptions. Ibuprofen or COX-2 inhibitors in heavy doses can wreak havoc on the stomach lining; too much acetaminophen may weaken the liver. Still, prescription medicine, used and monitored carefully, does help patients to "stay ahead of the pain." Since pain itself can debilitate the body and mind as completely as any drug dose might, there's no advantage in being able to boast that you can "tough it out" without help. Often the rule of thumb needs to be "moderation in all things."

Surgery might occasionally help. Sometimes procedures can successfully alleviate problems caused by specific nerve impingement issues or age-related changes in the joints. For people whose life is limited by their pain, it's worth considering, but always as a last resort.

That still leaves an array of nonsurgical treatments like cortisone injections, acupuncture, or homeopathic remedies, as well as physical therapy. It all takes time and effort. The best doctors are the ones who know their patients, understand their tolerance and limitations, and can develop an action plan. This assumes the patients cooperate and the doctors aren't too pressed for time.

I've done it all: anti-inflammatory medicines, injections, replacement surgery, and as much physical therapy as I'm allowed by my (luckily for me) decent health insurance plan. I've got a great doctor.

My pain, in other words, is manageable. I'm keenly aware that others aren't so lucky.

Even without the best available options (which we all deserve, but don't get me started), we might be able to manage our pain with some guidance. "Pain is both a sensation and an emotion," notes Francis Keefe, PhD, an associate research director at Duke University Medical Center, Division of Pain Management.[15] Since pain perception is amplified by fear and anticipation, we might be able to reduce the expectation that we're going to be hurting.

The blurred lines between what is physical, what is emotional, and what is a combination of the two is discomforting to some patients. Men in particular seem loath to try "touchy-feely" exercises (as one male friend referred to them) to reduce stress, for example. They seem more inclined to request "something for the pain" or "something to help me sleep." But chronic stress is dangerous to the body and the brain, overloading it with "powerful hormones ...intended only for short-term duty."[16] Chronic stress kills brain cells. Knowing that alone should be enough to slow down anyone's breathing (once one's heart stops racing).

The mind/body connection was brought home to me in an unusual fashion—not because of yoga or meditation or biofeedback or Buddhism, but because I had to give blood. As far back as I can remember, I've become lightheaded whenever I had blood drawn. My first recollection was as a nine-year-old, which I think may have been my first time. Just after leaving the doctor's office, I lost sight, literally. Everything went dark. "Mom," I whispered in terror as we entered the elevator, "I can't see." My mother went into mother mode, which is to say she pushed my head down between my legs and popped a piece of candy in my mouth. By the time we arrived at the lobby, I was still lightheaded, but my vision was restored.

After that, I went to every blood test and every invasive procedure with a piece of candy or some fruit juice. I explained to the doctor or phlebotomist that I had to get the sugar into my system the second she finished so I wouldn't keel over.

A few years ago, before major surgery, I had to give a lot of blood. The process took forty-five minutes; and when the needle was removed, one of the nurses noticed my grayish complexion and basement-level blood pressure and rushed over with a can of apple juice. I apologized for not warning her earlier about my physical symptoms.

"It's in your mind, you know," said an older nurse who was watching from the corner.

"No," I protested. "It's a physical problem. I become light-headed, my blood pressure drops, or my sucrose level or some-thing..."

"Your physical symptoms are real," she replied calmly. "But there's no physical *reason* for your reaction."

"So wait a minute." I sat up straighter, my dizziness abated, my pride forgotten. "You're saying my problem is psychosomatic?"

"I'm saying," she said with a smile, "you're scared sick."

I took a few days to process this new piece of information. From then on, I never again felt lightheaded after giving blood. Mind over matter has its limits, of course. Conquering fear, breathing deeply, and maintaining a positive outlook aren't in and of themselves cures. Not every pain can be willed away. People with debilitating illnesses hurt more often than not simply because their bodies are constantly assaulted by physical symptoms that naturally set off the brain's alarm system. We might assume aspirational messages of hope and optimism wouldn't help in these instances.

We'd be wrong. Corrine proves it.

I've known Corrine for eight years. She's always been in some respects a typical young woman, devoted to fashion, and as interested in various forms of virtual communication as are her friends. But Corrine isn't typical. She was born with a rare genetic skin disorder, recessive dystrophic epidermolysis bullosa. Normally our skin is held together by a type of collagen protein in the skin's fibers. The disease causes fibers to go missing or fail. Skin sloughs off and painful fluid-filled blisters form. In serious cases, blisters also appear in the esophagus, the upper airways, the stomach, and the intestines. Swallowing is difficult. Tooth decay is common, as is hair loss. In more severe versions of the disorder, fingers and toes may fuse together, the result of incomplete healing following chronic blistering. The blisters can also rupture, threatening an already compromised immune system. Life-threatening secondary infections may occur. Even the corneas may tear. There is no cure.

Corrine's case is severe. She's only twenty-five years old.

Independence has always been critical to Corrine so she's "fought harder" for it. She has her own apartment not too far from her family, but just far enough. She commutes two days a week into New York from central New Jersey to work at a clinic. Corrine graduated college with the rest of her classmates a few years ago, an amazing feat, considering her frequent illnesses and numerous operations to replace and repair her epidermis. A helper comes every morning to change the protective bandages she must wear to guard against injury or infection. This will not change; it's part of the rest of her life, as are more surgeries and more potentially life-threatening illnesses...but only a part.

Is it easier, I ask her, now that she's more mature?

"It's easier and harder as you get older," she says. "Easier because you understand the care you need, and what you have to do. You can soldier on more than when you were a kid. But at the same time you're also more aware of your limitations."

She's been willing to take on her own care, but she has learned to ask for help if she needs it, even if she doesn't want it. "It's about finding the balance," she tells me. "Was it more important to get what I wanted out of life and not worry about my pride in asking for help—or would I miss school and miss getting out?" The answer is clearly the former, as evidenced by the life-plan she's set for herself.

Making plans, she believes, keeps her mentally and physically healthy. To that end, she's applied to graduate school, hoping to pursue a degree in the medical field and help families and children enduring various illnesses. "If I'm not busy, it's not good," she notes with amused understatement.

The American Chronic Pain Association recommends patients to "set realistic goals and chart progress toward them."[17] They refer to practical accomplishments: Today I got up and walked around the block, or yesterday I was able to sit up myself. I think realistic goals can expand to include whatever we need in order to achieve an acceptable quality of life. Corrine's goals stretch even farther into the future. She owns her pain, but it doesn't own her.

Having a disease—any disease—is a struggle. More often than not, it becomes a battle in which only one side is presumed to triumph. In truth there are no winners and losers when it comes to disease. You don't *triumph* over your condition. Neither can you let it dominate you. You don't ignore it, nor do you give in to it. You work on it. You *manage* it, so you can manage your life.

My mother maintained an admirable optimism about her deterioration. She used to say she believed in mind over matter. Then she'd trot out the old joke that if you don't mind it doesn't matter. She always seemed cavalier about her pain. She was probably like many of her generation in that she didn't see the point of a prescribed exercise program or physical therapy. I found it ironic that my creative, imaginative mother couldn't—or wouldn't—see that the mind/body connection wasn't about which was in charge, the mind or the body. Admittedly, her arthritis was relentless. It attacked her hands first, so that she had to stop painting, and then her feet, so that she stopped moving. She gained fifty pounds, her discs compressed, she moved less. Then came one stroke and then another. She ended up immobile in a wheelchair. Was the progression inevitable? Maybe. Could it have been postponed? I wonder.

I began to exhibit symptoms of degenerative joint disease, my mother's *bête noir*, in my early forties. The first time I received the diagnosis, I was furious. "Are you telling me I have an old person's disease?" I demanded of my doctor. At the same time, I set out to learn everything I could about what it might mean for me. I'd watched my mother's deterioration and determined to do the opposite. I pledged relentless devotion to every sport I could manage for as long as I could manage. Eventually I learned to distinguish between what was advisable for me to do and what was not. No more tennis. Ice the sore joints. Wrap the ankle, rest the neck, wear the wrist brace on occasion, sit up, sit back, stretch. It's doable, especially when I have something to do.

Anyway, the upside is I'm now old enough that my symptoms are part of the normal litany of complaints my generation might have. I'm finally growing into my condition. If anything, I feel better.

Everyone handles pain and illness in his or her own manner. I'm as prepared as anyone I know to manage my own. I'm not perfect, but I do what I can and then some. The benefits are immediate; I feel better when I move. I sometimes joke that I'm crumbling, and my x-rays and MRIs bear me out to a certain extent; but I've become a big fan of targeted exercises. Can I halt the progression of the degeneration? Nothing on the horizon suggests I can. I might be able to slow it down, though, and that's become my goal.

People with more demanding disorders have to make decisions I don't have to face. Those with autoimmune diseases, for example, are presented with the option of taking drugs that suppress the immune system. No matter what your doctor tells you, that's a scary thought, especially when a drug advertises that a particular product has caused death by liver failure.

You roll the dice and you take your chances, right? No, you make as informed a decision as possible while asserting your absolute right to feel comfortable about your choices. My primary physician is careful about promoting particular pharmaceutical solutions. She knows she can't choose what's tolerable to me; she can only make recommendations. She's exactly right. Only I can decide what I can accept and what I'm willing to risk. Some doctors become offended if the choice you make isn't the one they offer. I don't care. While I don't advocate an adversarial relationship with one's physician, I do believe in making yourself clear. Because even when it doesn't seem as if you're in the driver's seat, you are.

Hope may not involve certainty, but it does involve choice and the choice has to begin and end with us as patients and as people. One way of turning the pain into something we control is to ask not what makes us feel worse but what makes us feel better. It could be as simple as standing up from the computer or going for a walk. It could be as complicated as pushing ourselves in a new direction or dedicating more time to breathing and relaxation exercises. Visualization used to seem like a silly technique to me (Imagine you're on a beach? Oh, please), but I've come to understand it's another way to imagine what could be. In fact, chronic pain management seems to incorporate C.R. Snyder's pragmatic approach to hope: Identify the aspiration, set the goals, and work toward them. Remain flexible and focus on the interim accomplishments along the way.

Dr. Oz is optimistic about pain treatment going forward. "We are in a pain renaissance,"[18] he declares. His enthusiasm is enough to make anyone feel good about the future, especially when he points to new discoveries that set that stage for new treatments.

At the end of the day, it still comes back to the balance Corrine mentioned. There may yet be days when the image of a wheelchair looms large in my mind. I'm always reminding myself I'm not my mother, at least not when it comes to either her symptoms or her choices in dealing with them. I have become devoted to Pilates. I also make an effort to get out, see friends; laugh out loud, I recognize my limits and I try to cultivate my assets, such as they are. Maybe the stubborn streak inherited from my dad will come in handy someday, if it hasn't ready.

And Corrine, what does she do? "Sometimes when I'm lying in bed at night I'll see snapshots of myself in the future, whether it be me bringing my first child home, or getting the call that I got hired at my dream job—and I feel like that is what hope is, little moments where we allow ourselves to dream without censoring ourselves. It's those moments in the darkness by ourselves when hope manages to shine through."

That's the prescription I'd most recommend.

Notes

1 Science Daily, "Why Women."
2 Institute of Medicine, "Relieving Pain."
3 Forman, "Gender Gap."
4 Minerd, "Extra Fibers."
5 Park, "Healing."
6 Ibid.
7 Institute of Medicine, "Relieving Pain."

8 National Academies, "IOM Report."
9 Park, "Healing."
10 National Institute, "Chronic Pain."
11 Oz, "End of Ouch?"
12 Gagné, "Pain."
13 Preidt, "Childhood Depression."
14 Marten, "Chronic Pain."
15 Laliberte, "Natural-Born."
16 Franklin Institute, "Stress."
17 American Chronic Pain Association, "Learned."
18 Oz, "End of Ouch?"

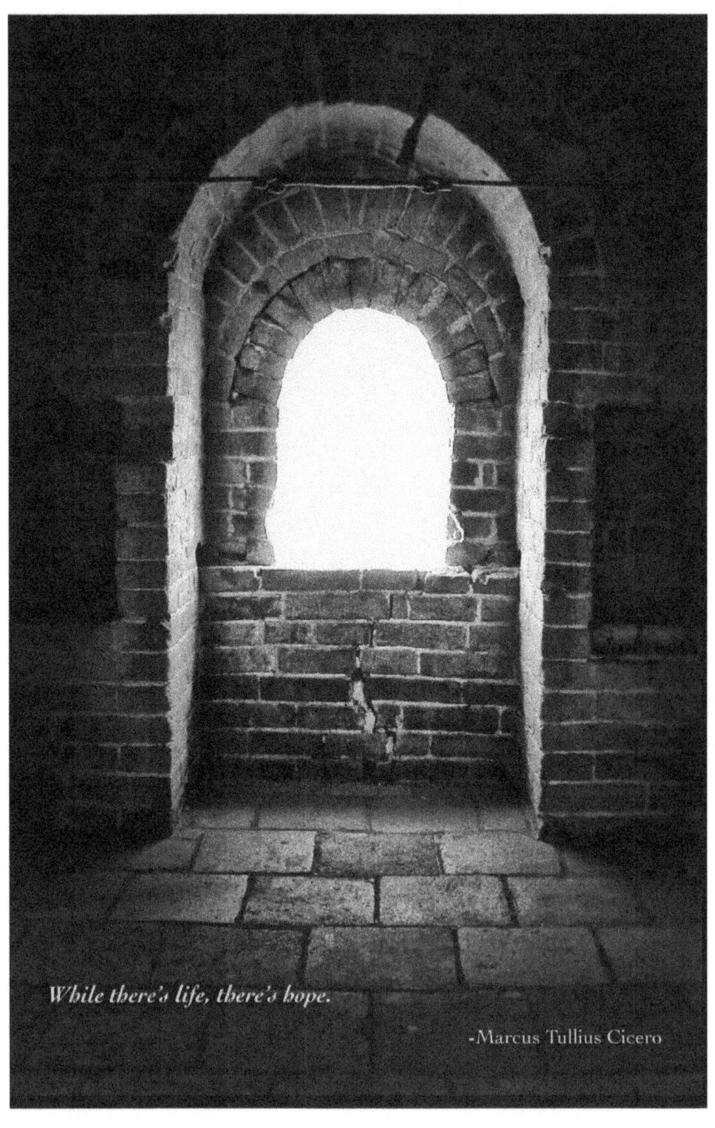
While there's life, there's hope.
-Marcus Tullius Cicero

CHAPTER 8

End of the Line

I'm not afraid to die. I just don't want to be there when it happens.
–Woody Allen

I see dead people. We all do. It sounds morbid; but honestly, we can't avoid it. We're exposed to the dead and the dying all the time—on television, in the news, in fiction, and in real life.

A number of us have undoubtedly witnessed death firsthand. We've felt the nearness of death as witnesses or as survivors. I didn't see my husband die, but I saw the blackened hole that had been the floor where he worked. I could see where he must have been. Certain details became important to me, like how big, how hot, how fast? Supplemented by ever-present images of burning towers, my imagination supplied what I couldn't see. It all played in a continuous loop in my mind, until one day it didn't. Those who suffer from posttraumatic stress can't shut off their mental tape.

No, none of us needs help in picturing death.

I think about death because it's played a prominent role in my life in recent years. My husband died, my parents died, my friends are beginning to die. Unless I live another sixty years (which seems unlikely), I'm quite beyond halfway through my life and on the downward slope. These thoughts can be pushed aside on a sunny day or ignored over a glass of wine with friends. They always return. Yet I'm not obsessed by them. It's a little unnerving not to know what death might feel like or when it might visit. But I don't obsess about it, just as I have no sense of what follows. It could be anything, which is to say reincarnation, paradise, or conversion into pure energy and a free trip around the universe. In any case, death doesn't terrorize me—at least not my own.

Dying is another matter.

The manner in which we come to the end of our lives is often incremental, measured in what we lose. It can be painful, limiting, and in some cases, time-consuming, just as we're running out of time. I've often wondered, as an observer, how hope could be helpful or even possible at the end of the line. Even more unnerving, the newest version of old age allows us to prolong life using the latest medical technology. Whereas my parents and others in their generation thrilled to the possibility of living past eighty, my friends expect to. Yet the quality of life past eighty varies widely and medical intervention doesn't always produce the best outcome.

Longer is not always better.

If hope is about looking forward, what part of dying can any of us look forward to except what is clearly out of our control: a painless decline and a peaceful death?

I've had some personal experience with this issue, as have most of my peers. My dad was identified with a life-threatening disease the doctors predicted would eventually kill him. It did, more or less, but not until he defied the odds for fifteen years. These were not worry-free years by any means. Dad endured several operations, twenty-three hospital stays, and at least a half-dozen near-death events. In that period of time, he also managed to travel to Africa and to Burma with my mother, play golf with friends, and win "best in class" for his stamp collection. The trips were both interrupted—the first by dad's illness, the second by my mother's injury; but really, how many eighty-year-olds get to these places? My father drove his beloved convertible until two or three years before his death. He walked nearly every day. The last year was physically hard, with all manner of occurrences that understandably scared him. Yet the most disturbing aspect of his pre-death was his fear of dying. He had horrible nightmares. Some were induced by his medical condition, and some were no doubt the product of mental machinations we couldn't imagine.

Thanks to luck, good fortune, and my sister's attentiveness, my dad was cared for at home. He was made to feel as if he retained some control. Still, his awareness of his decline was palpable, and when we took away the keys to his car, he felt utterly trapped. Dad always hoped and maybe even expected he'd die as his father had: suddenly, in the office after playing a round of golf. Instead, my father spent his last year in and out of the emergency room until he finally surrendered to the inevitable.

My mother proceeded to her end in a far more depressingly linear fashion. Her stress in dealing with my father's long-term illness, along with her painful arthritis, probably contributed to the series of small mini-strokes and related "episodes" that wore her down. She managed to accompany my father on their last trip to Africa with plans (or so she told us later) to jump with him off the top of Victoria Falls. Instead she stumbled and fell at the bottom. The best laid plans, I guess.

Robbed of movement and the ability to string together complete thoughts, she spoke little and endured much. My father grew deaf and refused a hearing aid. His need for more sound was at odds with my mother's long-standing sensitivity to sound. Guess who prevailed? Worse, his terror at his decline (along with his disease) caused him to rage. His tirades increased, as did her helplessness in the face of his fury. They had a great marriage, don't misunderstand me; but she was without control and as much a prisoner of her environment as he was of his.

No wonder she seemed to keep her eye on the exit. She talked about death with longing, even asking us to push her off a balcony or get her pills she might swallow in lethal doses. Yet in the manner of long-married couples, she was determined to hold on until my father was gone. In this she was ultimately successful. We brought her north to a nursing home immediately after his death. We gave instructions to keep the television off and the classical radio station turned low, and asked the aids to speak quietly to her (both orders were frequently ignored; nursing homes assume cacophony is comforting to all their patients). We brought in an art therapist to work with her and took her out several times a week. Nevertheless, Mom died ten months later. Her primary job, caring for and caring about my father, was done. She'd waited for nature to take its course. One winter up north was all it took.

There's nothing uncommon about my parents' last years. My friends and I share stories about dementia, despair, anger, and frustration that feel depressingly similar. Coming off my husband's death, I may have imagined life was far worse for my parents than it really was. They were together and, for the most part, at home. For all their travails, my parents had a truly symbiotic relationship. They would have preferred not to be sick, of course, but they were made as comfortable as possible and I like to believe they knew it.

Of course I worry about what will happen to me in old age. If I think my parents had a hard time in their last years, what will I face as an elderly single?

It's not promising. In a series called "The New Old Age," *The New York Times* reported on a surging divorce rate among baby boomers that will send more of them into old age alone. With marriage rates falling for the next generation, the number of single elderly people is expected to rise sharply. The article then sounded the alarm: "The elderly, who have traditionally relied on spouses for their care, will increasingly struggle to fend for themselves. And federal and local governments will have to shoulder much of the cost of their care. Unmarried baby boomers are five times more likely to live in poverty than their married counterparts, statistics show. They are also three times as likely to receive food stamps, public assistance, or disability payments."[1]

Great, more to worry about.

There's very little about aging that pleases Susan Jacoby. In her fierce book, *Never Say Die*, she focuses her forceful intellect on the false marketing of old age. Jacoby writes from a deeply personal place. The death in middle-age of her romantic partner, her struggles with an aging parent and her own impending sixty-fifth birthday did not leave her with the sunny picture of aging as a happy, productive time.

The long-predicted wave of baby boomers (by the year 2030, they'll make up nearly twenty percent of the US population[2]) has pressured gerontologists to create subcategories according to chronology: "young old," "old," and "old old" are now used divide those over sixty-five into discrete groups.[3] Jacoby introduces some disheartening data concerning the oldest group. For instance, she cites statistics that show those beyond eighty-five with a fifty percent chance of living in a nursing home. This group also exhibits a much higher incidence of Alzheimer's disease than does the broader category of people between sixty-five and eighty-five.[4] Maybe it's not surprising, but it doesn't make living longer particularly appealing.

Like Ehrenreich, Jacoby believes relentless positivity about illness and old age blinds us to evidence. Getting old is not about how "we can beat this thing," she argues.[5] We accuse anyone who suggests a brake on unrealistic expectations as "ageist." Ninety is not the new fifty, Jacoby counters sharply, adding, "In real old age, as opposed to fantasyland, most people who live be yond their mid-eighties can expect an extended period of frailty and disability before they die."[6] The golden years are far more tarnished than we might want to believe.

Jacoby's critique of our unrealistic expectations supports earlier observations by the renowned author and surgeon Dr. Sherwin B. Nuland. In his bestseller 1993 book, *How We Die*, he notes, "The fact is death is not a confrontation. It is simply an event in the sequence of nature's ongoing rhythms."[7] Neither Nuland nor Jacoby urge oldsters to "shuffle off the stage of life for the convenience of the young."[8] However, Nuland reminds us, "There is a framework into which all levels of pleasure and accomplishment fit—and pain, too. Those who would live beyond their nature-given span lose their framework."[9]

Rumblings about a looming generational conflict are escalating as baby boomers retire in unprecedented numbers. True, the new old might be better informed and in better shape. They might be productive, if they choose to, and if society allows them to be. If they're healthy, or can remain relatively so, why shouldn't the elderly keep on keeping on? Most people I know are desperate to contribute in some manner, rather than become a drain on civic or family resources. I can't be certain my friends represent the norm, however. Perhaps the boomer majority wants to kick back and collect Social Security and use other government programs. My generation is already caricatured in the media as collectively sharing a sense of entitlement. Maybe we'll insist on being treated in ways that will help future generations—or maybe we won't. Is a generational fight inevitable?

The premise of Albert Brooks' darkly funny book, *2030: The Real Story of What Happens to America* is that a cure for cancer and other medical advances have made it possible for almost everyone to live into their nineties. The storyline has it that resources are stretched to the breaking point by those "olds," as anyone over seventy is called. Young people, in this dystopian future, are having a very difficult time supporting themselves and their families. Unrest is growing. One of the subplots concerns the U.S. president's ninety-four-year-old mother who is being kept alive and in a coma. There's no hope she'll ever wake up, but the people who run the for-profit and amenities-rich care center aren't about to change their marketing plan. They're in the business of warehousing wealthy if comatose patients. They make a bundle feeding off the hopes of families who can't bear the thought of losing their loved one.

Cynical, yes, but Brooks is writing satire. He's also finding the absurdity in our apparently natural urge to hang onto life by our fingernails, whatever the (monetary or emotional) price. Jacoby's anger isn't so much directed at our impulses as at a healthcare system that dictates "aggressive steps should be taken to extend life at any cost."[10] The oldest people aren't given a true picture as to potential complications following particular procedures, she insists. She's right about that, although we patients and decision-makers are complicit in refusing to consider complications. Give me the surgery, we may insist of our physicians; I'll take my chances. Many of us don't even like to talk about quality of life and its alternatives. My father wouldn't consider suspending efforts to bring him back from his near-death experiences. He never signed a Do Not Resuscitate (DNR) order. Families who watch their loved ones slip away often panic and may insist on extraordinary measures without thinking about how hard extreme intervention can be even on a healthy body (anything from a broken rib to an injured esophagus). One element of the original Affordable Care Act plan allowed doctors to offer older and seriously ill patients a range of end-of-life treatment choices. The backlash was astounding; some feared the elderly would be "encouraged" to choose inexpensive medical options. Such is our inability to face death with any kind of equanimity that we would confuse being informed with being railroaded into making a "bad" or fatal decision.

"It is reasonable, not heartless, to raise the question of whether just remaining alive, as long as expensive medical procedures make it possible, is a worthy goal," Jacoby insists.[11] I agree. Older patients should be able to make their own decisions about whether they find their quality of life tolerable and when they might want to end their own. They don't deserve to be second-guessed, nor do their friends or relatives warrant criminal prosecution for trying to assist. I support recognizing and treating depression in the elderly, as long as we also take into consideration other factors. For example, if an older person is depressed about being in a nursing home, there's probably something about the nursing home experience we need to improve. I also propose that giving ill or elderly patients as much control as possible over the manner of their deaths can actually inject a bit of hope into late-stage living.

But what if we could live longer, decades or more beyond our predicted lifespan, thanks to some discovery that alters our very cells? Jacoby presents the arguments put forth by both anti-aging researchers and evolutionary biologists, who often find themselves opposing one other over the ethics of prolonging life. She then reminds us, "Our society has to this point failed miserably in attempts to work out the serious social and economic problems by the 'old old' in the present."[12]

Not much hope there.

While I understand Jacoby's anger with the way we market happiness and health in this country, I'm not convinced that she's painted an entirely accurate portrait of old-age attitudes. The story she relates about her grandmother, who suggests the worst thing about living too long is feeling useless to anyone, rings true. Perhaps, as Jacoby writes with stinging bluntness, her death truly was "a release from a purgatory worse than any circle of hell."[13] I sometimes wonder whether my mother felt the same way. No one should live beyond his or her time, as Jacoby says, and we can question whether medicine makes that possible without making it optimal.

Most of us want to stay alive as long as possible. How can we judge whether someone's time is up, unless we are that person? Many of my baby boomer friends have made declarations like, "If I can't do such and such anymore (read, walk, feed myself), just shoot me." More of us are putting end-of-life directives in place. Most people who go into nursing homes want to leave alive. Unfortunately, that isn't usually what happens. Perhaps that's why "Never put me in a nursing home" is a commonplace command issued from older parent to adult child.

Jacoby is absolutely right; we haven't addressed the problems of aging, even for those with financial means. I'm not thrilled with the geriatric care presently offered. It appears we suffer from a deficit of sympathetic, forward-looking doctors and a paucity of imagination when it comes to providing stimulating, socializing environments for our old. The respect factor plays a role. We honor the spry ninety-year-olds who look and act like Betty White did at ninety because her aging makes us hopeful. Yet the idea that a diminished or debilitated person at that age has anything to offer still doesn't occur to us.

What goes around comes around, of course; and making the lives of people in their last years both easier and more enjoyable may become a priority in our culture. After all, there will be more of us oldsters. I don't mean to suggest grandparents will live with their progeny, although multi-generational living arrangements will always be with us. Many of the "new old" don't have the same degree of family ties, however. Others living alone want to continue living alone. What most people I know want is some sort of companionship—access to friends and neighbors. Coupling may be less important than socializing as communities become the ideal way to provide physical and emotional support.

The idea is to age in place, albeit with home designs that are kinder to older people—single-level, open floor plans with easy-to-reach shelves and appliances. Builders and planners have become interested in alternatives to senior housing. The current crop of plus-fifty-five communities that cater to "active seniors" falls short of serving the oldest; my parents, for example, were never more isolated than when they found themselves in such a place, over eighty and ill.

Some newer communities that have attracted investment are deliberately multigenerational, where an assisted living center coexists with daycare facilities or schools, all within walking distance of shops. Another trend is college town retirement communities, which affiliate with major universities, allowing older people to attend classes and lectures. One almost retro design development geared to facilitating interaction is the front porch. According to a spokesperson for Ecumen, a Minnesota nonprofit senior housing and services company, "What we're seeing in America is a growing reverse from isolating seniors to integration across ages" and the developing of communities where "aging is pretty much just a number."[14]

That 's still an exaggeration. Remember, ninety isn't the new anything, except ninety. Nevertheless, any reversal of the marginalization of the majority of older people is welcome. Increased visibility of our oldest has another benefit; it might allow society to (once again) find some level of acceptance, if not respect, for the idea of aging.

Old age will happen to all of us (unless we die before it does). Jacoby's concern is that society simply isn't prepared to take a realistic view of what that means. In order to be seen as someone who is aging successfully, she notes in her introduction, we are told never to "complain about health problems to anyone younger, weep openly for a friend or lover who has been dead for more than a month or two, admit to depression or loneliness, express nostalgia for the past (either personal or historical), or voice any fear of future dependency."[15] If we can't be open about our fears, both she and Ehrenreich are saying, we risk feeling even more isolated at a time when we can most benefit from understanding companionship.

Our insistence on projecting an upbeat attitude isn't tied exclusively to discomfort with old age or illness. We don't like to feel vulnerable. We shy away—at times, far away—from being reminded about life's underbelly: addiction, troubled youngsters, cheating spouses, chronic grief, chronic pain, chronic unemployment, the monster that is someone else's boss, or the beast that exists in someone else's mind. Unless we have a professional stake in someone else's problems, it's probably a bad idea to immerse ourselves in another's difficulties. On the other hand, a little empathy can go a long way.

Realistically, we need to plan for old age. This doesn't assume we know what to expect, but that we consider what we might need. Living wills, while not universally respected, go a long way in making our wishes known. As to advice about embracing aging, I'd hasten to add "as best we can." Crabby days are to be expected. Older people who stay connected to others, even when they're ill, have a better quality of life. Yes, illness isolates us, but so does pride. My parents didn't want others to see them as they failed. They turned down company far more than they sought it.

Planning is not the same as hoping, a friend of mind told me, and Jacoby agrees. "At eighty-five, only a fool...can believe the best years are still ahead," Jacoby fumes.[16] I'd argue she hasn't accounted for the way our perception of life changes. We tend to revise what is acceptable, accommodating to our slowing bodies and minds. Some studies have suggested many older people are happier. What cognitive changes take place to produce this mood is unclear; research is ongoing. However, psychologists hypothesize that happiness among the elderly is self-starting. They're inclined to "seek out situations that will lift their moods," or "hew their goals toward greater well-being."[17]

We live until we die, and we do so best if we have something to look forward to. Making light of diminished expectations is a problem younger people have when looking at what it means to get old. If you used to be a prima ballerina or run marathons or give lectures at a university, even if you held a job and raised a family, what's so great about looking forward to a good night's sleep or an excellent meal? To which I might reply, what's so bad about it? Maybe the anticipation of a nice experience doesn't count as hope in most people's minds, but I might be happy to take it.

Or not. I might indeed feel differently about the business of living at eighty-five than at sixty-five. At some point, quality of life will diminish. That is the nature of our existence and it's why, as I indicated earlier, control over one's life ought to mean the freedom to say "enough."

Giving the elderly, never mind the terminally ill, the ability to end their lives or seek assistance to do so is controversial. We Americans don't like the idea of self-induced death. This may stem from the conviction that death is God's business (or nature's business) and not ours. We do tend to reverse ourselves when it comes to employing extraordinary measures to prolong life. Suddenly the natural course of events isn't the right one. Honestly, we don't like to let go or say goodbye. That's perfectly understandable. Further, we often assume the elderly don't have their own best interests at heart. It's part of a distressing trend to "infantize" older people. But just as some might need better diagnosis or treatment or care or attention, others may be perfectly capable of deciding to end their lives with grace and dignity. Isn't it reasonable to grant to our oldest citizens that privilege, with safeguards in place?

If I'd been legally allowed to give my mother some sort of gentle poison, I would have. She told me she was miserable. I believed her. On the other hand, what if we could have found an ideal environment that would let my parents live together, but with access to some sort of social life and at least some of the things they loved?

I don't know. What, after all, is a "good" death? To a warrior, it means dying victorious on the battlefield, with all the attendant honor, glory, and love of nation. To others, it might mean dying on the job or in bed while asleep. Most of us would prefer a quick death, or one that involves an easy, gentle slide, without pain and without fear.

I choose to believe I might have more options than a sadly diminished life or a self-induced death, at least for the foreseeable future. My friend Jane turns eighty-five next year. A successful artist, she continues to exhibit her work. She also belongs to a group of women who are determined to stay in close proximity to one another and to the things they both enjoy (theater, museums, movie houses) and need (hospitals, physical therapy). Other groups (again mostly women) are working with builders to come up with an affordable housing solution that includes communal dining and carpooling or other forms of transit. Changing attitudes about end-of-life options offer some hope that we can live agreeably until the moment of our deaths.

"The older I get, the more determined I am that my life get larger, not smaller," a friend wrote me. The message, while inspirational, runs counter to everything we understand about how old age reduces us. Fortunately, I've come to know people who understand how much work it takes to accept limitations while expanding opportunities. Even more fortunately, they prove to me both how necessary and how much fun it is to do that work.

Meanwhile dying seems to go on forever, unless we die young. Eventually, we all reach the end of the line. Even though my father was ill for fifteen years, he lived a good life, filled with books and conversations, adventures, and studies. He read up until his final heart attack; he was forever stretching his mind. He complained, but I don't think he was sad, not really.

As for my mother, she had two or three very bad years, but how much of a lifetime is that—three or four percent? The rest of her days were filled to the brim with the things she told me she'd always wanted and finally gotten: her family, her art, and a sixty-four-year personal and professional partnership with my father. Even in the last decade, she spent time reflecting, remembering, and coming up with much to be proud of and few regrets. When she finally found the peace she sought for her dying—the hushed stillness and filtered sunlight of hospice—she appeared as angelic and beautiful as I can remember.

Notes

1 New York Times, "Divorce Rates."
2 Census Bureau, "Next Four Decades."
3 Transgenerational Design, "Characteristics."
4 Jacoby, *Never Say Die*, 12.
5 Ibid., 6.
6 Ibid., 12.
7 Nuland, *How We Die*, 10.
8 Jacoby, *Never Say Die*, 26.

9 Nuland, *How We Die*, 87.
10 Jacoby, *Never Say Die*, 26.
11 Ibid., 25.
12 Ibid., 261.
13 Ibid., 3.
14 Reuters, "Ecumen."
15 Jacoby, *Never Say Die*, xiii.
16 Ibid., 5.
17 Science Daily, "Older People."

Every time you stand up for and ideal, you send forth a tiny ripple of hope.
-Robert Kennedy

CHAPTER 9

ON PURPOSE

Since we do not know the future, we should choose the view most likely to improve it.
–Susan Neiman

The *New York Times* online has a section called "The Stone" which is devoted to all sorts of lively philosophical, epistemological, ontological, ethical, and existential discussions. I'm a follower; I read the articles by greater and lesser-known philosophers as well as the comments that follow. These people are smart. They're knowledgeable and well-read, these writers and their philosophers. All of them have strong views on the meaning of life and what may or may not follow.

I have to admit, when I'm asked to contemplate the meaning of life, I get flummoxed. Suddenly I've got questions, although they may not be typical of most seekers. First I ask, What *is* the meaning of life? But then I wonder if there's supposed to be a meaning? Does there *have* to be one? Are we expected to know what that meaning might be? Are we entitled to know? What does meaning mean? You can see how easy it is to get sidetracked, at least for someone who chronically questions.

Trying to parse the philosophical and moral implications of human life has merit. For one thing, it can inform many of our ethical decisions. Yet knowing the how or why of our presence as sentient human beings doesn't seem as pressing to me as it might to others who feel more anxious about finding those sorts of answers. I'm curious about how the universe began, but I don't worry there may be a grand design that imparts a universal meaning I've somehow missed.

Wondering about the meaning of life isn't the same as wondering about a life of meaning or how one might go about living it. Even though we may not know *why* we're here, we can do something meaningful *while* we're here. Some may argue this is nothing more than verbal sleight of hand, soothing palaver to distract us from larger issues. But what's more important than dealing with what we have here and now? Psychologists and neurologists both tell us depression is linked to "a diminished or absent sense of meaning and purpose."[1] Conversely, purpose is a mood elevator. This leads me to believe that whether or not we can ever truly know the meaning of life, we clearly need *our* lives to mean something

Separating purpose from the ultimate question about why we're here presents a conundrum. How can we live lives of meaning unless we understand the big picture and can see exactly where we fit into the whole? We chafe at our inability to know. We insist that lives of meaning must be tied to a quantifiable larger purpose. Even if that purpose is a closely held secret never to be revealed, it must exist. But where?

Religion seeks to provide the most clear-cut answer to the "meaning of life" puzzle. God is often described as the whole into which we fit, and through whom we may understand what our lives mean. This is the premise of *The Purpose-Driven Life*, a best-selling book by Rick Warren, pastor of a mega-church in California. On his website, Warren describes his book as helping readers to "understand God's incredible plan for their lives, [enabling] them to see the big picture of what life is all about and begin to live the life God created them to live."[2] Warren lists five purposes, all of which come directly from God: worship (because we were planned for God's pleasure), fellowship (because we were formed for God's family), discipleship (because we were created to become like Christ), ministry (because we were shaped to serve God), and evangelism (because we were made for God's mission).

The message seems to be: Here are the rules; follow them. Here's the community; join it. The rest is taken care of.

I'm always amazed at the confidence religious leaders express in their ability to know exactly what God wants from us; how certain they are that they can faithfully representing his intentions to millions of congregants. These pastors and imams and priests ignore or discount the fact that the divine texts from which they derive their inspiration were written by men of a different time and culture with human biases and constituencies of their own to answer to. Some followers of the present-day religious leaders may believe, as did their ancestors, that a life dedicated to these man-made scriptures is imbued with both purpose and hope. Many more, I suspect, simply can't figure out how to access hope without religion, so they accept the necessity of dogma and "cherry pick" from among the proffered beliefs. For instance, my friend Jan, who belongs to a Unitarian congregation because it's "relatively dogma-free," has assured me, "We Unitarians must be the only religion without hope." I'm convinced most Unitarians wouldn't want to hear their community described in that fashion. I suspect she's referring to divinely inspired hope and suggesting that without dogmatic certainty, there's no hope.

Perish the thought. If religion insists purpose derives from certainty in God's plan, extreme positivism turns each of us into mini-gods. Empowerment is the driver of this purpose-driven life. I encourage any mind-set that helps overcome feelings of victimization. I also favor trying to make things happen and support the concept of personal responsibility. But I'm as leery of inviolate human power as divine power. We're not invincible, nor are we masters of anyone's universe, even our own. Ignoring or denying our limitations is not merely delusional; it can also be dangerous.

Neurologist Robert Burton asserts that certainty isn't required in order to reach a positive mental state, but purpose is a biological imperative "as necessary as hunger and thirst...for survival."[3] Obviously neither purpose nor hope can cure disease or render us immortal. But that doesn't make either of them worthless, not at all. Purpose comes from having a reason to get up in the morning, hope follows, and our lives are vastly improved. It's a perfectly reasonable, even a worthy goal for us to have.

How, then, do we find purpose?

Oftentimes, *purpose* is imagined in terms of some sort of majestic vision or noble goal. It doesn't need to be quite that grand to infuse a life with meaning. We don't have to lead a revolution, discover a cure for cancer, devise a means to end poverty, or foster dozens of children. If we want to make a contribution, we can give money or give of our time. We can join groups or reduce our carbon footprint. We can learn and exchange knowledge. Social networking doesn't have to be relentlessly self-centered; part of its charm for me is that it encourages us to pass all sorts of information back and forth. We can spread joy or be joyous, be a teacher or a student. Purpose is available in a wide assortment of shapes and sizes. It's a great motivator and a natural pain suppressant.

I have friends who think defining purpose in such a manner is both small-minded and pointless. "Sharing an article from the *Times* on Facebook is not purpose," Ann the researcher states categorically. "And I'm not leading a life of purpose just because I help someone find information on the Internet or make a new friend."

I beg to differ. I come back to a wonderful piece of writing by a dear friend of mine who goes under the name "Cartouche" on occasion. She wrote, "I want to evolve into this person who digs deeper and [recognizes] that there is nothing more important, more worthy or noble than to be of service to mankind. I aspire to be able to leave a little bit of humanity better off than when I arrived... I want to find the courage, strength and determination not only to figure out how I can go about accomplishing this, but to embrace the fact that *not* doing it is not an option."[4]

The above was inspired by a video she saw about a man who helps feed the hungry. I know Cartouche's life has changed quite a bit since seeing the video. She's moved, co-edited a well-received cookbook, and taken a new job. Maybe she isn't yet involved with feeding the hungry of the world and maybe she won't be. I know her writing has inspired other people to look within themselves for their inner "good guy" and to find ways large and small to contribute to making the world a better place.

In *Moral Clarity: A Guide for Grown-Up Idealists*, Susan Neiman lays out a way to approach the idea of purpose without certainty. A purposeful life guided by moral principles, she observes, doesn't require the "passivity of religion that promises peace in the hereafter."[5] Neiman's value system is deeply steeped in Jewish tradition, and her book contains a number of references to Old Testament stories. Nonetheless, her viewpoint is distinctly earthbound. She sets out to illustrate that meaning can be found not by submitting to whatever comes along, but by working to achieve a life based on Enlightenment values she highlights: happiness, reason, reverence and hope.

I admit I struggle with the word "reverence." If Neiman means "appreciation," I'm there. If we're talking about a cosmic "It," I hesitate. I was nonplussed when Burton, whose wonderful book deserves a much wider audience, suggests our sense of purpose might be tied to something "beyond us that needs to be acknowledged."[6] I've self-identified as "spiritual but not religious" without knowing what I believe that to mean. I alternate between wondering how specific I need to get with my understanding that we may not be all there is (or we may), and wanting desperately not to insult whatever is out there. I even find myself hesitating in yoga class when asked to express gratitude and bow down to the divine within us. I respect the power of both the known and the unknown. I'm just not certain who I ought to be thanking, let alone bowing to.

In the last few years, I've become aware of a method by which I can acknowledge goodness and beauty without assuming or denying anything necessarily *caused* it, especially anything I might be called upon to bow to. This approach is known as *mindfulness*, and it has a couple of terrific advantages. By training ourselves to *pay more attention* to what is around us, we can expand our perceptions; we can see more. Our senses become attuned to our surroundings, deepening the experience, and giving new insights into what we're observing. The *novelty* of what we're seeing more carefully has been shown to excite the dopamine neurons and increase gray matter density in the brain.[7] Mindfulness can also acknowledge the emotion we might feel when viewing a majestic sunset or hearing a stirring piece of music or a baby's laughter.

Awareness produces both physical and psychological well-being. It's something my late husband, a science geek at heart, always tried to demonstrate to me. "Look," he'd say, pointing to a night sky or to a hint of growth among the fallen trees in the woods on a March afternoon. "Don't just stare; see if you can tell what's happening." I don't think he meant for me to see changes on a cellular level. Rather, he wanted me to notice the remarkable truth of nature: deadfall becomes host to new life. I'm still amazed how intuitively he grasped not only the importance but also the pleasure that comes from observing the known world. What a lucky man he was!

The Roman poet Lucretius knew all about mindfulness. His *On the Nature of Things* is a cornucopia of observations about the natural world delivered in lush, often sensuous language. *On the Nature of Things* promotes the teachings of the Greek Epicurus, who first put forth the idea "that everything that has ever existed and everything that will ever exist is put together out of indestructible building blocks, irreducibly small in size, unimaginably vast in numbers."[8] Stephen Greenblatt, whose book *The Swerve* celebrates the rediscovery of Lucretius' lost work, marvels that the poem's "scientific vision of the world—a vision of atoms randomly moving in an infinite universe—was in its origins imbued with a poet's sense of wonder," a wonder that doesn't depend on "gods and demons and an afterlife" but rather on the recognition that we are made of the same matter as the stars and the oceans and all things else."[9]

Incidentally, both Epicurus and Lucretius believed pleasure-seeking was a worthy goal. Although deliberately misunderstood by critics, their pleasure was not of the hedonistic variety but came from living a full life that allowed for friendship, philanthropy and happiness and involved the pursuit of peace of mind. Imagine if we could direct our ever-striving, guilt-ridden, self-critical selves to such a purpose. It'd be like paradise on earth.

Our current guru of mindfulness has got to be the celebrity astrophysicist Neil deGrasse Tyson. His celebration, his sheer joy in what remains to be discovered is contagious. It's hard to single out any single quote from this eminently quotable man but I loved what he said in a recent interview with an author from *Hemisphere Magazine*, noting that the atoms in our bodies can be traced to the atoms that formed the galaxy we live in: "This fact tells us that not only do we live in the universe, the universe lives within us."[10]

That's enough to inspire reverence in me.

It's inevitable increased awareness will also take in everything that's *wrong* in the world. We're not fools, and most of us realize how much we can't fix or even absorb when we're buried under an avalanche of bad news. Who doesn't say, from time to time, "What's the point of life? It's cruel, it's random; it ends." The point of separating questions about the meaning of life from how to make our lives meaningful is so we can understand that one is not dependent on the other. Creating a purposeful life provides human beings with positive benefits. It doesn't really matter what life's purpose is.

We're learning more and more each day about what

we don't and can't know, which almost sounds paradoxical. Dr. Burton the neurologist reminds us that feeling we know something has nothing to do with either certainty or knowledge. In fact, the limits of our brain in processing and storing information have brought into question the notion of free will. Are we actually capable of making independent decisions? Neuroscientist Michael Gazzaniga, the author of *Who's In Charge: Free Will and the Science of the Brain*, suggests it's unlikely. Eventually, he writes, "... we will get over the idea of free will and accept we are a special kind of machine, one with a moral agency which comes from living in social groups."[11] Sam Harris, author, atheist and scientist agrees. In *Free Will*, he states bluntly, "Free will is an illusion. Our wills are simply not of our own making."[12]

Well, great. If I don't have control over my choices, why should I do anything at all? Why set goals? Why identify a purpose? Why hope?

For one thing, the argument about free will hasn't been "settled" yet. Philosophers contributing to "The Stone" still argue passionately that it's not a false construct, depending on how we understand it. Others insist the absence of free will doesn't negate the importance of our ethical decisions, or any decisions at all. As Sam Harris wryly notes in *The Moral Landscape*, "If I had not decided to write this book, it wouldn't have written itself."[13]

We all share experiences that can help us come to a consensus concerning right and wrong. From time to time, we even rely on our instincts to help us. We may learn some day that we have a lot more control than we thought in this decade or century, or that we've evolved to gain more control. We may also discover our reality resembles the whimsical last minutes of the original *Men in Black* movie—that our entire universe is nothing more than a bocce ball in the playground of some unimaginably large creatures.

Don't give it another thought—seriously.

Science doesn't generally engage in philosophical questions about the purpose or meaning of life. Scientists work with evidence and develop theories. That evidence accumulates and either reaffirms the scientists' conclusions or, in some instances, alters the original theory. This has unfortunately led to a widespread misunderstanding of a scientific theory as mere speculation. Scientific inquiry may be about questioning, but it's not about guessing. Science focuses on discovery and possibility. As a non-scientist, I've learned to appreciate how energetically science actually promotes both purpose and hope.

How so? Science provides answers. Science also trains its eye on what is unknown. We humans like solutions and conclusions. Science works toward giving us both. Modern technology in particular addresses our need for certainty by letting us know when the files will be copied, when the subway train will arrive, when our team's timeout will end, and when our favorite show will resume. It bends to our obsession with countdowns whose outcome we can predict. But science knows the journey may not always lead to the definitive answer. Some things resist confinement into "discrete, bounded blocks of time."[14]

Nick Paumgarten, writing in *The New Yorker*, demonstrates how elusive that finish line can be in practice. He introduces us to a "never-ending" experiment Australian scientists are keeping alive. The test was originally designed by a physics professor in 1927 to demonstrate viscosity in fluids to his class. The professor poured hot pitch into a glass funnel and allowed it to cool, so that the students could see how long it took the fluid to move. The cooled pitch didn't release a single drop for eight years. The second drop came nine years after that. From then on, every ten years or so (more or less, no one can say precisely when the drop will fall), the pitch releases one drop. The imprecision thrills the scientists who are keeping track. "Unpredictability is one of the great things about nature," enthuses the experiment's current guardian, John Mainstone.[15]

Unpredictability, uncertainty, the exception to the rule, the anomaly—these are realities on which science thrives. Susan Neiman also celebrates uncertainty, finding in it the seeds of possibility. Possibility feeds her version of hope. Hope is possible precisely because we don't know for certain how things are going to turn out. In that case, why not plan as if they might turn out well? Logic, she insists, can just as easily support a positive outcome as a negative one. It's the glass half empty/half full paradigm. What's important to our well-being is that we work toward worthy goals. The worthiness of those goals is determined by us. All we need to do is look around and see how we can make things better. We may succeed beyond our wildest dreams; we may not. The planning gives meaning to the journey. The journey becomes as significant as the destination. We may not be able to guarantee a happy ending for ourselves or for mankind as a whole, but we can use whatever talents we have in the pursuit of the best possible outcome.

Existing research supports the idea that some sort of purpose creates a more interesting and rewarding life. We can hold onto notions of certainty in the face of mounting evidence that many things about which we're certain are illusory. Or we can decide that, absent proof that we're either the most important thing in the universe or slaves even to our own brains, we don't need to plan or hope for anything.

There's another version that says since we don't know, why not live a life that makes us *feel* relevant, useful, directed, and meaningful? As to whether it makes any difference, we'll know when we get there. Or not. In the interim, we've lived a good life.

It's difficult to define a purpose-driven life in broad strokes. The American Humanist Association's newest mission statement "affirms our ability and responsibility to lead ethical lives of personal fulfillment that aspire to the greater good of humanity."[16] That's as good a purpose as any I can think of. The AHA also uses as a slogan "good without God." That may cause discomfort among the faithful but it needn't be interpreted as an insult. It's just to say goodness, purpose and hope don't require instructions from above.

The point is: God is beside the point. At least that's how I read it. Still offensive to some, I'll grant you. I like that the slogan urges us to put our energies into the lives we are given, however they are given, and to live without certainty but with plenty of possibility and opportunity...and room for hope.

Whether we're the largest, smallest, most or least significant thing in the universe makes for a marvelous late-night discussion. It's not relevant to how we live in the here and now. We need to look around, take measure of ourselves, and decide what we can do and how much of it we do to improve our lives and the lives of as many others as we can reach. Like Cartouche, I'm committed to the idea that happiness lies not in hindering, but in helping. The help doesn't need to be measured by us or by anyone else. We do what we can do. We have no magic powers and no one-size-fits-all set of rules that will deliver unto us a ready-made, purpose-driven life. For that, we may have to rely on our own gifts.

Notes

1 Burton, *Being Certain*, 179.
2 Purposedrivenlife.com, "About the Book."
3 Burton, *Being Certain*, 183.
4 Cartouche, "Living."
5 Neiman, *Moral Clarity*, 75.
6 Burton, *Being Certain*, 182.
7 Heller, "Slowing Down."
8 Greenblatt, *The Swerve*, 75.
9 Ibid., 8.
10 Wright, "Neil deGrasse Tyson."
10 Cook, "Neuroscience."
11 Harris, *Free Will*, 5.
12 Ibid., 105.
13 Paumgarten, "Countdown."
14 Ibid.
15 American Humanist Association, "About Humanism."

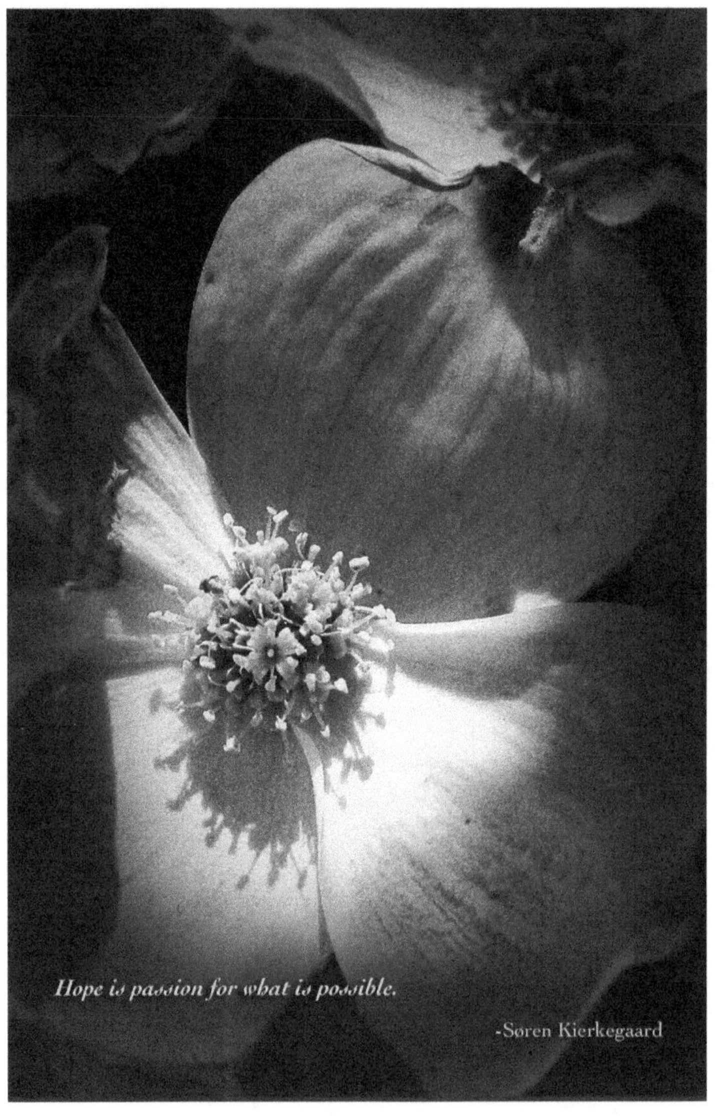
Hope is passion for what is possible.
-Søren Kierkegaard

CHAPTER 10

Practically Happy

To make progress, we need to be able to imagine alternative realities—better ones—and we need to believe that we can achieve them.

–Tali Sharot

I'm sitting on a bench with a cup of coffee and a book. The air is warm and moist; a velvety summer blanket that rests lightly on my shoulders. The palm tree to my left leans over ever so slightly, as if to read along; the ferns remain still except to shift in the breeze created by the opening and closing of doors...

Wait; what? Where am I? Is this some sort of visualization exercise and if so, why didn't I add a beach?

Mastering the art of visualization is a goal of mine, but not one I've yet achieved. If I manage to shut out the world around me for a brief moment, I can sometimes summon the feeling of sand between my toes or a warm waft on my face. I just can't quite be there, meaning, at the shore.

I can be in the moment, however. So I've chosen to spend a little time in the greenhouse-like corridor outside my doctor's office. I find the idea of a warm tropical atmosphere one of the more innovative and appealing aspects of this otherwise ordinary office complex. While I haven't made a special trip just to treat my sinuses and my psyche, I've arrived early to my appointment in order to enjoy a moment's break from the dim, gray midwinter afternoon. It's no day at the beach, but it's a nice treat.

Last year, I sat on a real beach and alternately watched the sunset and the people around me working on their various electronic devices. "It's beautiful, isn't it?" I whispered to my neighbor, a gentleman intensely focused on his glowing smartphone.

"Yeah, I guess," he responded without looking up. "There'll be another one tomorrow."

Maybe there'll be another email/text message/eBay auction/ news alert/video or chat tomorrow, I thought...or not. His priorities and mine weren't aligned on that beach, so I sat back and enjoyed the view.

It did occur to me that in order to look forward to anything, even for one day, one would need to look up, or at least look around.

Back to the non-beach, outside the doctor's office: if I can't be at the ocean, I can summon a feeling of contentment. I wonder, is this happiness?

One common definition explains happiness as a "state of well-being characterized by emotions ranging from contentment to intense joy."[1] As pleasant as it is, I don't assume the feeling will last, although I do assume (I hope?) it can and will return. Most of us believe we want to be happy, but there may be biological reasons why we shouldn't maintain that state. The eminent scholar and best-selling author, Robert Wright, has pointed out that evolution doesn't support a permanent state of happiness.[2] The lack of fulfillment, he explains, is what keeps us motivated. I suspect the founding fathers, pre-Darwin, somehow knew that, which is why the Constitution guarantees only the *pursuit* of happiness, not the thing itself. Nonetheless, there is an entire field dedicated to the study of happiness. A leading "happiness" scholar, Paul Dolan, suggested in an interview with *Fast Company* that we take note of what truly makes us happy and make sure we have a life that allows it to happen. I know; if it were that easy, everyone would be doing it. [3]

Yet some people do appear to reach that blissful overall state of mind. Do they take steps to be happy or do they put themselves in situations that add to their happiness? Maybe there's a happiness gene or an innate bias toward being happy, if not all the time then most of it.

People who describe themselves as happy have ties to communities of one sort or another. They have friends with whom they share stories and activities, with whom they commiserate, gossip, laugh, or cry. This is as true of kindergarteners as it is of the elderly. Greater happiness is reported among those who consider themselves religious. A recent study suggests that their well-being may, in fact, derive as much or more from a sense of belonging than from belief in an all-knowing deity.[4] In any event, a community of like-minded friends provides both structure and ritual, whether it involves the annual church picnic or the Sunday meet and greet.

Online networks provide a version of community. For people whose physical movements are circumscribed, social networking is a lifeline. Even so, it's easy, in the day of electronic connections and virtual communities, to undervalue human interaction. The death of my spouse brought to light my semi-isolation (working from home, spending time strictly as a couple), which may be why I consciously involved myself in 9/11-related activities for a time. It was a shock to be around so many people, and not just because of the traumatic shared experience. It turned out I wasn't practiced in the art of socialization. Even now, a number of friends and acquaintances later, I still have to push myself out the door. Practice makes, if not perfect, then at least connected.

That's not to say my friends don't bring me joy; they enrich my life greatly. My years as a (gulp) widow have actually revealed the possibility of belonging to a number of communities, each with its own set of rituals. I bought a dog several years ago for companionship but she has resulted in my "membership" in a group of neighborhood dog-owners. We routinely run into each other in the morning or evening and stop to chat about everything from our dogs to politics. Some of us now socialize without our dogs, but make no mistake about it; the canines form the nexus of our group.

I'm also part of a loosely constructed group of women, some married, some single, some retired, some working and all "of a certain age" who live in my town. We hold potluck suppers every other month. Many of us attend local functions (I live in a college town with lots going on). Some of us volunteer at a local women's shelter. These are not things I would have done on my own, I admit—and I realize, too, that women tend to form friendships and gather together much more readily than do men.

Epicurus knew what he was talking about when he defined happiness in terms of friendship.

Being happy doesn't require a jammed social life, of course. There are many ways to achieve a sense of well being, from finishing a project to discovering a new interest. I feel content in my bed with my dog and a good book. I experience a little zing of pleasure seeing the first crocus every spring. Some people's happiness comes from familiar routines or possessions. I probably have to count myself as one of them. Stability is often the most precious gift we can give our most vulnerable members of our society—children, the elderly, and those who are frail or disabled. It's not the same as certainty, however.

The world is filled with people who seem to derive pleasure from the certainty that whatever they or their friends believe is what is right to believe. I don't doubt either the strength or the sincerity of their convictions, these certain people. Beliefs provide an anchor, a starting point on which we can build both our moral foundation and our outlook. The problem with belief is that it can become hard, inflexible, immoveable, no longer righteous but self-righteous. Imagine a tree that doesn't bend when the wind comes. Now imagine the wind is change (not hard; just think Bob Dylan's iconic song Blowing in the Wind). A tree that doesn't bend is more likely to fall over. So no, I don't trust most unshakeable convictions to supply me with happiness or to protect me when change inevitably rolls around.

I don't mean to suggest we have to live looking over our shoulders, watching what we do or say, waiting for the other shoe to drop. We don't and we can't, not if we want to enjoy ourselves in this life. No one would opt for change when things are going well, but change is what we get—change in our lives and in the lives of those closest to us and, one would hope, our understanding of what's going on around us and within us. Change isn't about whether we control it or it controls us. Change is rather something we have to accept.

I'm not a big fan of change, I have to admit. I remind myself, especially when I have too much time on my hands, not to look back with any sense of yearning. My subconscious mind doesn't yet obey; but for now, I have to accept that my mind has a mind of its own.

Accept. How I used to hate that word. I equated it with resignation. They feel one and the same when we're young (or not so young) and restless; when we're told to wait until we're older or get more experience or can understand the world into which we've been born. Me, I couldn't stand the idea of limitations. I felt as if to accept them was to resign myself to a less interesting, less fulfilling, less happy life.

Oddly enough, I began to separate acceptance from resignation when I was introduced to the Serenity Prayer through a friend's involvement with Alcoholics Anonymous. Attributed to the theologian Reinhold Niebuhr, (although the sentiment may have antecedents in the writings of early Buddhist scholars), it takes the form of a request:

> *God, give us grace to accept with serenity the things that cannot be changed,*
>
> *Courage to change the things which should be changed, and the Wisdom to distinguish the one from the other.*[5]

I never paid much attention to the words because, well, I assumed it was a prayer to some sort of external being. Even if we drop the word "God," we're still asking for help from someone, aren't we, some external force that has the power to give us what we need? And if we don't get that help, has that someone or something then let us down? Have we missed the signals or messed up our request? Have we failed ourselves? It's hard to feel serene when one is castigating oneself.

Try changing the emphasis from who is being petitioned to what is being sought. Suddenly this prayer or poem or whatever becomes both more inclusive and more instructive. What does the petitioner need? She needs serenity, courage, and the wisdom to distinguish between the two. How does she get to that point? She *accepts* what she can't change, so she doesn't have to *resign* herself to hopelessness.

What a great life lesson! Or maybe we should say, What an impossible task! We are doomed to struggle with questions about the meaning of life. James Wood, reviewing *The Joy of Secularism: 11 Essays for How We Live Now*, noted that neither religion nor atheism is comfortable with questions about why life is so short and so random: "Religion assumes that they are not valid questions because it has already answered them; atheism assumes that they are not valid questions because it cannot answer them."[6]

So, yes, we'll worry and wonder, toss and turn, and face doubt and fear in turn. That's also an acknowledgment that such thoughts are a part—but not the whole—of what it means to be alive and as fully sentient as evolution and science allow us to be. We can always draw comfort from accepting (that word again!) that, as the writer F. Scott Fitzgerald said, "The test of a first-rate intelligence is the ability to hold two opposed ideas in the mind at the same time, and still retain the ability to function."[7] True, Fitzgerald was detailing his spiritual and physical exhaustion following his heyday as a brilliant but reckless writer. No one ever guaranteed that a fully open mind wouldn't also, at times, feel the pain of the stretch.

That's the key, isn't it? There are no guarantees. For some odd reason, I don't find that distressing at all. Expectation *isn't* the same as hope. Expectation, like certainty, is inflexible. Both *demand* a particular result. If we don't achieve that result—poof!—there goes hope. But resilient, renewable hope succeeds, because it's adaptable.

Hope, even in the smallest amounts, requires faith. I'm not talking here about the certainty of religious faith but rather faith in the possible, not the probable or the likely; not the deserved or expected, and not the "wait for it" variety. The version of faith I'm thinking about also requires us to believe what is best about the human spirit. Right away, I'll lose many of my more cynical readers who may swing their arms in wide arcs and ask me to take in the miserable world as it is, and "get real." My neighbor, a smart, tart-tongued woman with strong views, nearly gagged when I told her I was writing about hope in small doses. "You can't be serious," she exclaimed. "How can you believe in *any* kind of hope?"

Oh, but I do. In fact, I'm prepared to explain and defend my version of hope in small doses, caveats, modifiers, and all. It reflects my deepest belief in accommodation and in the power and strength of flexibility. People have to do what they have to do to get through life. I don't want to be miserable or afraid, nor do I want anyone else to feel that way. I know from experience that misery is no fun. What I want to do is share my conviction (yes, it is a conviction) that hope and happiness are possible without certainty. Frankly, I'm tired of being told *might* or *could* or *possibly* or *perhaps* are equivocations and therefore weak, just as I'm tired of being told an agnostic is hedging her bets. I have no bets out there, people. When I say, "I don't know," I mean it. I'm all about discovery. Uncertainty gives me permission to stay open to possibility.

Uncertainty has certain advantages, pardon the pun. It makes a fine dance partner for flexible hope. We may not know, but we can pursue knowledge. We may not find, but we can search. There's always something new to learn and learning increases brain activity, which might preclude age-related diminishment. We may even accept the limitations of our brain and still ask questions. Who's to say otherwise? I don't see embracing the journey rather than the destination as accommodation to anything except the realities of life.

Hope doesn't require that we give ourselves over to a higher power, or to the idea that we can become life's master manipulators. This is to say that as sentient beings, the best way of getting through—no, more than getting through, *living* life as fully as possible—is to quit worrying about what can't be known, and focus instead on what can be done. This applies to us whether we're working on a cure for cancer or trying to survive it as best we can.

Have I created the "perfect" recipe for workable hope, one that will allow for uncertainty, permit doubt, promote happiness, stay grounded in reality, and encourage imagination? (Insert big sigh here) Not quite...or not yet...or not sure. I do have a working manifesto, subject, as is life, to revision.

I understand the near-universal longing for answers to the puzzle surrounding thought and feeling, existence and purpose. I identify with our need for stability and balance. Although I'm beginning to enjoy big-picture uncertainty in the abstract (I'm becoming a "glass half full" kind of person), I tend to play it safe when it comes to my well-being. I'm *sensible*. I could stand to become a bit less so.

Still, I choose hope, at least in small doses. I choose to *assign* myself a purpose, and embrace the journey that leads to the fulfillment of that purpose. I acknowledge the risk of stumbling along the way, of never completely accomplishing what I set out to do, or of discovering that I inadvertently changed course. I accept as a working theory that humans live their best lives when they ascribe meaning to their lives. I take as a matter of faith that it is within each of us to live meaningful lives, to love, to interact, to connect in fellowship; and that *how* long our reach, or wide our influence, is far less important than the path we set for ourselves. I realize I will always feel some disappointment and may come to conclusions and discoveries late in life that I wish I'd reached earlier. But so what? That only means I've been growing and learning. It also means I'm human...and being fully, completely human is always going to be my most important accomplishment.

I don't propose to know how hope will continue to fit into my life. I only know that in some small measure, I want it. I need it. I deserve it. We all do.

Notes

1 WolframAlpha, "Happiness."
2 Wright, "Dancing."
3 Segran, "Happier Life."
4 Healy, "Study."
5 Niebuhr, "Serenity Prayer."
6 Woods, "Is That."
7 Fitzgerald and Wilson, *Crack-Up*, 57.

Acknowledgements

Thanks to Humanist Press, which originally published this book and for the excellent work of its publisher/editor Luis Granados. Thanks also to Marly Cornell, whose initial editing expertise was invaluable.

Applause all around for the evocative photography by artist Cherie Siebert, which adds immeasurably to the meaning and quality of the book.

Finally, special thanks goes to my sister and friend, Deborah Stern. From cover design to layout to first and last proofs, she's been the one to help me stay true to my vision. I know she isn't yet sure what her workable version of hope looks like, but I know she'll get there.

About the Author

Nikki Stern is an author who writes political, social and cultural commentary at www.nikkistern.com. Her first book, *Because I Say So: the Dangerous Appeal of Moral Authority*, details her experiences as a 9/11 widow and looks at the larger cultural context that supported (and still supports) unequivocal moral certainty. Nikki has written pieces for the *New York Times, Newsweek, USA Today, Humanist Magazine, Princeton Magazine*, and online at *Salon*, *TruthOut*, and *Talking Writing*. She has appeared on NPR's "All Things Considered" and CBS Sunday morning, among others.

Nikki served as the first executive director of Families of September 11 (FOS11), a national advocacy and outreach organization. Under her leadership, FOS11 received an award from the conflict transformation group Search for Common Ground. She's published a novella, *Don't Move,* and is working on a novel set in New Orleans. For more, visit http://nikkistern.com

About the Photographer

Cherie Siebert hails from three generations of photographers. She works in a variety of media. Most of the images for this book were shot using an iPhone 4s. For more information on Cherie and her work, see http://artfish.com

Bibliography

"About Humanism," American Humanist Association. http://americanhumanist.org/Humanism

"About the Book, *The Purpose-Driven Life*," 2010. http://purposedriven.com/books/pdlbook/#purpose

AP Stylebook (aces2012). http://twitter.com/#!/APStylebook.

"Borg," *Startrek Database*. http://www.startrek.com/database_article/borg.

"Changing Minds," http://changingminds.org/.

"Characteristics of an Aging Population," *Transgenerational Design Matters*, updated 2009. http://transgenerational.org/aging/demographics.htm.

"Correspondence Regarding the Templeton Foundation," https://whyevolutionistrue.wordpress.com/2009/06/21/fighting-back-against-templeton/

"Difference Between Hope and Faith," http://www.differencebetween.net/miscellaneous/difference-between-hope-and-faith/

"Divorce Rates Among Boomers to Reshape Old Age," *The New York Times*, 2 March 2012. http://newoldage.blogs.nytimes.com/2012/03/02/divorce-rates-among-boomers-to-reshape-old-age/?ref=health.

"Ecumen Discusses Intentional Multi Generational Communities and the Evolution of Senior Living," *Reuters*, 23 February 2011. http://www.ecumen.org/blog/future-senior-housing-not-senior-housing-what-do-you-think#.VRrFPpPF8mc

"Feelings of Hope Create Striking Brain Effects That Could Help Alleviate Serious Afflictions Like Pain, Parkinson's Disease, and Depression, Researchers Report," press release, Society for Neuroscience, 15 November 2005. http://www.sfn.org/Press-Room/News-Release-Archives/2005/FEELINGS-OF-HOPE?returnId=%7B0C16364F-DB22-424A-849A-B7CF6FDCFE35%7D

"Happiness," WolframAlpha. http://www.wolframalpha.com/input/?i=happiness

"Hope," *Free Dictionary*. http://dictionary.reference.com/browse/hope.

"Hope," *Merriam-Webster*. http://www.merriam-webster.com/dictionary/hope.

"Hope," *Oxford Learners Dictionary*. http://www.oxfordlearnersdictionaries.com/us/definition/english/hope_1

"IOM Report Calls for Cultural Transformation of Attitudes Towards Pain and Its Prevention and Management," *The National Academies*, 29 June 2011. http://iom.edu/Reports/2011/Relieving-Pain-in-America-A-Blueprint-for-Transforming-Prevention-Care-Education-Research/Press-Release-MR.aspx

"Relieving Pain in America: A Blueprint for Transforming Prevention, Care, Education and Research," *The Institute of Medicine*, 29

June 2011. http://learn.fi.edu/learn/brain/stress.html

"Researchers Demonstrate How Placebo Effect Works in the Brain," *Physorg.com*, 30 July 2007. http://www.physorg.com/news105029324.html.

"Stress on the Brain," The Franklin Institute. http://learn.fi.edu/learn/brain/stress.html

"The Next Four Decades: The Older Population in the United States 2010- 2050," United States Census Bureau, May 2010. http://www.aoa.acl.gov/Aging_Statistics/future_growth/DOCS/p25-1138.pdf

"Wave of Brain Activity Linked to Anticipation Captured," *Journal of Neuroscience*, 26 February 2009. http://explore.georgetown.edu/news/?ID=40182&PageTemplateID=295

"What is Chronic Pain?" *National Institute of Neurological Disorders and Stroke*, 28 December 2011. http://www.ninds.nih.gov/disorders/chronic_pain/chronic_pain.htm.

"What We Have We Learned," *American Chronic Pain Association.* http://theacpa.org/what-we-have-learned

"Why Are Older People Happier?" *Science Daily*, 6 January 2012. http://www.sciencedaily.com/releases/2012/01/120106135950.htm.

"Why Women Get More Migraines Than Men," *Science Daily*, 6 August 2007. http://www.sciencedaily.com/releases/2007/08/070806094703.

htm.

Asimov, Janet. "Accepting Uncertainty," *Humanist Network News*, August
2011. http://americanhumanist.org/HNN/details/2011-10-accepting-uncertainty

Bohen, Halcyon. "Treating the Chronically Disappointed," *Family Therapy Networker*, 1 January 2000.
http://www.ucdenver.edu/life/services/counseling-center/Documents/Treating-the-Chronically-Disappointed.pdf.

Borba, Dr. Michele. "Depression and Kids," *Reality Check*, 12 June 2011.
http://www.micheleborba.com/blog/2011/06/12/depression-hits-kids-as-young-as-3-what-to-expect-age-by-age-parenting/.

Borchard, Terese. "Twenty-One Ways to Overcome Disappointment," *Beliefnet.com*, 15 April 2010.
http://www.beliefnet.com/Health/Emotional-Health/2010/03/21-Ways-to-Overcome-Disappointment.aspx.

Burton, MD, Robert A. *On Being Certain You Are Right, Even When You're Not*. New York, NY: St. Martin's Press, 2008.
http://www.rburton.com/_i_on_being_certain_i___believing_you_are_right_even_when_you_re_not_63166.htm

Cartouche. "Living Your Life on Purpose," *Cartouche's Blog*, 15 December 2010.
http://open.salon.com/blog/cartouche/2010/12/15/living_your_life_on_purpose

Cole, Brian Paul. "Correlations between trait and academic measures of hope and the Inventory on Learning Climate and Student Well-Being," October 2008.

http://gradworks.umi.com/14/50/1450456.html.

Colihan, Kelley. "Does 'Hope Therapy' Help Depression?" *WebMD*, 18 August 2008. http://www.webmd.com/depression/news/20080818/does-hope-therapy-help-depression

Cook, Gareth. "Neuroscience Challenges Old Ideas About Free Will," *Scientific American*, 15 November 2011. http://www.scientificamerican.com/article/free-will-and-the-brain-michael-gazzaniga-interview/

Dreifus, Claudia. "Life and the Cosmos, Word By Painstaking Word," *New York Times Magazine*, 9 May 2011. http://www.nytimes.com/2011/05/10/science/10hawking.html?pagewanted=all&_r=0 n

Edmonds, Molly. "What is Hope," *How Stuff Works*. http://people.howstuffworks.com/what-is-hope.htm

Edwards, Jim. "Big Pharma's Next Big Thing: Anti-Psychotic Medicines for Pre-Schoolers," *Citizens Commission on Human Rights International*, 9 September 2010. http://www.cchrint.org/tag/joan-luby/.

Ehrenreich, Barbara. "Overrated Optimism: The Peril of Positive Thinking," *Time Magazine*, 10 October 2009. http://content.time.com/time/health/article/0,8599,1929155,00.html

Ehrenreich, Barbara. *Bright-Sided: How Positive Thinking Is Undermining America*. New York, NY: Metropolitan Books/Henry Holt & Company, 2009. http://books.google.com/books?id=qR3qwimbnO8C&dq.

Euripides. *Iphigenia in Taurus*, translated by Gilbert Murray, Project Gutenberg, http://www.gutenberg.org/cache/epub/5063/pg5063.txt.

Eustice, Carol. "What is the Placebo Effect?" *About.com*, 6 October 2011. http://arthritis.about.com/od/arthritistreatments/g/placebo.htm.

Feigenbaum, Eric. "The 1920s: 'Sell Them Their Dreams,'" VMSD, 3 May 2001. http://vmsd.com/content/the-1920s-sell-them-their-dreams.

Fitzgerald, F. Scott, and Wilson, Edmund. *The Crack-Up*. New York, NY: Charles Scribner's Sons, 1931. http://books.google.com/books/about/The_Crack_up.html?id=B8saLwl-2TEC

Foreman, Judy. "The Gender Gap," *The Boston Globe*, 27 September 2010. http://www.boston.com/news/health/articles/2010/09/27/learning_why_men_and_women_experience_pain_differently/

Franklin, Benjamin. *Poor Richard's Almanac*. http://archive.org/stream/poorrichardsalma00franrich/poorrichardsalma00franrich_djvu.txt

Friedman, Richard A. "Like Drugs, Talk Therapy Can Change Brain Chemistry," *New York Times*, 27 August 2002. http://www.nytimes.com/2002/08/27/health/behavior-like-drugs-talk-therapy-can-change-brain-chemistry.html

Gagné, Jim. "The Different Kinds of Pain," website of Dr. Jim Gagné. http://www.jamesgagne.com/KindsOfPain.shtml.

Gray, PhD, Peter. "The Dramatic Rise of Anxiety and Depression in Children and Adolescents: Is It Connected to the Decline in Play and Rise in Schooling?", *Psychology Today*, January 26, 2010. https://www.psychologytoday.com/blog/freedom-learn/201001/the-dramatic-rise-anxiety-and-depression-in-children-and-adolescents-is-it

Greenblatt, Stephen. *The Swerve*. New York, NY: W.W. Norton and Company, 2011. http://books.google.com/books?id=SnQ_lQInytkC&dq.

Hahner, PhD, Kathryn. "Learned Helplessness: A Critique of Research and Theory," report in *Safer Medicine*, 1989. http://www.safermedicines.org/reports/Perspectives/vol_1_1989/Learned%20Helplessness.html

Harris, Sam. *Free Will*. New York, NY: The Free Press, 2012. https://books.google.com/books?id=iRpkNcRt1IcC&printsec=frontcov-er&dq=Free+Will&hl=en&sa=X&ei=7KAaVdSUF4nFggSqj4OwDg&ved=0CDEQ6AEwAA#v=onepage&q=Free%20Will&f=false

Havel, Váčlav. *Disturbing the Peace*, translated by Paul Wilson. New York, NY: Random House, 1986/1991. http://books.google.com/books/about/Disturbing_the_peace.html?id=_yToxN33RoAC

Healy, Michelle. "Study: Happiness is Having Friends at Church," *USA Today*, 7 December 2010. http://usatoday30.usatoday.com/yourlife/mind-soul/spirituality/2010-12-07-happyreligion07_ST_N.htm

Heller, Rick. "Slowing Down the Consumer Treadmill," *The Humanist*, July/August 2011. http://thehumanist.org/july-august-2011/slowing-down- the-consumer-treadmill/.

Hesiod. *Works and Days*, translated by Hugh G. Evelyn-White. http://www.sacred-texts.com/cla/hesiod/works.htm

Jacoby, Susan. *Never Say Die: The Myth and Marketing of the New Old Age*. New York, NY: Pantheon Books/Random House, 2011.
http://books.google.com/books/about/Never_Say_Die.html?id=LQtJbS92XD4C

Jamieson, Alastair. "Dogs Can Be Jealous, Say Scientists," *The Telegraph*, 7 December 2008.
http://www.telegraph.co.uk/science/science-news/3659416/Dogs-can-be-jealous-say-scientists.html.

Laertius, Diogenes. *The Lives and Opinions of Eminent Philosophers*. http:// www.forgottenbooks.org/info/9781440064067.

Laliberte, Richard. "Natural-Born Pain Killers," *Prevention Magazine*, June 2007.
http://paincenter.stanford.edu/press/external/2007-07prevention.pdf.

Lyubomirsky, Sonja. "The Happiness Diet," *Monitor on Psychology*, April 2008.
http://www.apa.org/monitor/2008/04/overthinking.aspx.

Marten, Sylvia. "How Chronic Pain Leads to Depression," *Spine-Health*, 21
February 2008. http://www.spine-health.com/blog/study-demonstrates-how-chronic-pain-may-lead-depression

Meade, Michael. "The Hidden Hope of the World," 11 August 2011. http://www.huffingtonpost.com/michael-meade-dhl/america-crisis-hope_b_919452.html

Mendez, Elizabeth. "In U.S., Optimism About Future for Youth Reaches All-Time Low," *Gallup Politics*, 2 May 2011. http://www.gallup.com/poll/147350/Optimism-Future-Youth-Reaches-Time-Low.aspx

Mills-Scofield, Deborah. "Hope is a Strategy (Well, Sort Of)," *Harvard Business Review*, 9 October 2012. https://hbr.org/2012/10/hope-is-a-strategy-well-sort-of.

Minerd, Jeff. "Extra Fibers May Heighten Female Pain Perception," *Med- Page Today*, 27 October 2005. http://www.medpagetoday.com/Neurology/GeneralNeurology/2017

Neiman, Susan. *Moral Clarity: A Guide for Grown-Up Idealists*. Orlando, FL: Houghton Mifflin Harcourt, 2008. http://books.google.com/books/about/Moral_Clarity.html?id=fbb2rcQD92cC

Niebuhr, Reinhold. "The Serenity Prayer." http://skdesigns.com/internet/articles/prose/niebuhr/serenity_prayer/

Niemi, Mag-Britt. "Placebo Effect: A Cure in the Mind," *Scientific American*, February 2009. http://www.scientificamerican.com/article/placebo-effect-a-cure-in-the-mind/

Nietzsche, Friedrich. *Human, All-Too-Human*. New York, NY: Penguin Books, 1994. https://books.google.com/books?id=ywHCXaThiJ8C&dq=All+Too+Human+Nietsche&hl=en&sa=X&ei=b50aVYKDJoShgwSyqIHABw&ved=0CCwQ6AEwAg

Norem, Julie K. *The Positive Power of Negative Thinking: Using*

Defensive Pessimism to Harness Anxiety and Perform at Your Peak. Cambridge, MA: Perseus Books Group, 2001. http://books.google.com/books/about/The_positive_power_of_negative_thinking.html?id=ttmv9xg2L70C

Nuland, Sherwin B. *How We Die: Reflections on the Final Chapter*. New York, NY: Vintage Books/Random House, 1993. http://books.google.com/books/about/How_we_die.html?id=ffjo3ghdnqwC

Oz, Mehmet. "The End of Ouch?" *Time Magazine*, 11 March 2011. http://content.time.com/time/specials/packages/article/0,28804,2053382_2053599_2053598,00.html

Paradiso, MD, PhD, Sergio. "Book Forum: How the Mind Works," *American Journal of Psychiatry*, 1 October 2002. http://ajp.psychiatryonline.org/toc/ajp/159/10

Paramount Pictures, *Forrest Gump*, 1994. https://www.youtube.com/watch?v=GCbUadfoCho

Park, Alice. "Healing the Hurt," *Time Magazine*, 4 March 2011. http://time.com/83461/healing-the-hurt/

Paumgarten, Nick. "Countdown," *New Yorker Magazine*, 2 January 2012. http://www.newyorker.com/talk/2012/01/02/120102ta_talk_paumgarten.

Plutchik, Robert. *Emotions and Life: Perspectives from Psychology, Biology, and Evolution*. Washington, DC: American Psychological Association, 2002. http://books.google.com/books?id=a0p4QgAACAAJ&dq.

Pope Benedict XVI. "Encyclical Letter 'Spe salvi,'" *ZENIT*, 30 November 2007. http://www.zenit.org/article-21152?l=english.

Preidt, Robert. "Childhood Depression, Anxiety Tied to Pain in Adulthood," *Azma.com,* 1 August 2011 http://www.azma.com/Asthma-Article.aspx?type=news&aid=758

Raskin, Richard. "Camus' Critiques of Existentialism," *Minerva*, Vol. 5, 2001. http://www.minerva.mic.ul.ie//vol5/camus.html.

Revson, Charles. http://www.brainyquote.com/quotes/quotes/c/charles-rev103182.html

Sahgal, Gita, "Conquering Fear With Hope: Secularism 2014," *Open Democracy,* 9 October 2014. https://www.opendemocracy.net/5050/gita-sahgal/conquering-fear-with-hope-secularism-2014

Sartre, Jean-Paul and Benny Lévy. *Hope Now: The 1980 Interviews*. Chicago, IL: University of Chicago Press, May 1996. http://www.press.uchicago.edu/ucp/books/book/chicago/H/bo3619055.html

Sartre, Jean-Paul. *Existentialism is a Humanism.* https://www.marxists.org/reference/archive/sartre/works/exist/sartre.htm

Segran, Elizabeth. "How To Intentionally Design a Happier Life," *Fast Company,* 15 February, 2015. http://www.fastcompany.com/3042346/my-creative-life/how-to-intentionally-design-a-happier-life.

Selegman, Martin and Maier, Steven F. "Failure to Escape Traumatic Shock," *Journal of Experimental Psychology*, Vol. 74, #1, May 1967.

http://psych.hanover.edu/classes/Learning/papers/Seligman%20 Maier%201967.pdf

Shakespeare, William. *The Rape of Lucrece*. http://www.online-literature.com/shakespeare/331/

Sharot, Tali. "The Optimism Bias," *Time Magazine*, 28 May 2011. http://content.time.com/time/health/article/0,8599,2074067,00.html

Snyder, C.R. *The Psychology of Hope: You Can Get There from Here*. New York, NY: The Free Press, 1994. https://books.google.com/books?id=dCWv9MYZ58oC&printsec=frontcover&dq=The+Psychology+of+Hope&hl=en&sa=X&ei=DJgaVburH8uigwTftYRg&ved=0CCwQ6AEwAA#v=onepage&q=The%20Psychology%20of%20Hope&f=false

Spiegel, Alix. "When It Comes to Depression, Serotonin Isn't the Whole Story," *NPR*, 23 January 2012. http://www.npr.org/blogs/health/2012/01/23/145525853/when-it-comes-to-depression-serotonin-isnt-the-whole-story

Stokes, Bruce. "Europe's Kids Are Moody and Depressed," *Pew Research Center,* 23 February, 2015. http://www.pewglobal.org/2015/02/23/europes-kids-are-moody-and-depressed/

Svartberg, Kenth. Tapper, Ingrid, Temrin, Hans, Radesäter, Tommy and Thorman, Staffan. "Consistency of Personality Traits in Dogs," *Safer Medicines.org*. http://www.svartbergs.se/pdf/Consistency_of_personality.pdf

Sweeney, Julia. *God Said "Ha,"* starring Julia Sweeney, Miramax, 1998. http://www.imdb.com/title/tt0119207/.

The Catholic Encyclopedia. "Hope," *The New Advent.* http://www.catholic.org/encyclopedia/view.php?id=5889

Verghese, Abraham. "Hope and Clarity," *New York Times*, 23 February 2004. http://www.nytimes.com/2004/02/22/magazine/22WWLN.html

Werner, Michael. "Humanism 101," *The Humanist*, November/December 2011.

Woods, James. "Is That All There Is?" *The New Yorker*, 15/22 August 2011. http://www.newyorker.com/magazine/2011/08/15/is-that-all-there-is

Wright, Chris, "The Hemi Q&A: Neil deGrasse Tyson," *United Hemispheres Magazine,* March 2015, http://www.hemispheresmagazine.com/2015/03/01/hemi-qa-neil-degrasse-tyson/

Wright, Robert. "Dancing to Evolution's Tune," *Time Magazine*, 9 January 2005. http://content.time.com/time/magazine/article/0,9171,1015866,00.html

Zimmer, Carl. "Human Nature's Pathologist," *New York Times*, 28 November 2011. http://www.nytimes.com/2011/11/29/science/human-natures-pathologist.html